Sales & Operations Planning in Software

Shaun Snapp

Contents

CHAPTER 1: Introduction...1

CHAPTER 2: The Relationship Between Planning Systems
                          and S&OP Systems..13

CHAPTER 3: S&OP Versus Integrated Business Planning 39

CHAPTER 4: SAP IBP, ANAPLAN & SAP Cash Management......................47

CHAPTER 5: The Impact of SAP IBP With HANA 67

CHAPTER 6: S&OP, Aggregation, and Forecast Hierarchies........................71

CHAPTER 7: Challenges In S&OP Implementation 87

CHAPTER 8: How Misunderstanding Service Level Undermines
                          Effective S&OP 105

Conclusion 117

References 122

Author Profile...125

Abbreviations 128

Links Listed in the Book by Chapter...129

CHAPTER 1

Introduction

Sales and Operations Planning or S&OP for short is the process by which sales, operations and finance collaborate in order to determine the planning activities on the part of the company. S&OP has the following attributes:

- *Connecting the Business:* S&OP is all about connectivity, binding the different branches of the company together, and ensuring compatibility between the most general of operating plans (top-level) and the most specific details of its execution (bottom-level).

- *High Level Planning:* S&OP is the second highest level of planning that a company does – second only to strategic planning.

- *Balancing Act:* S&OP helps the companies determine how to balance the orientations of sales, operations and finance and keep up with demand.

- *Capacity Treatment:* S&OP fuses supply-chain planning with forecasts for product demand, constantly evaluating the constraints of a company's supply chain and offering insight as to the costs of borrowing money to increase production. The central question then becomes: will capturing increased demand generate enough revenue to justify the increased cost?

- *Aggregation:* S&OP should be an aggregated form of planning, although as we will see in this book several software vendors push S&OP towards a very detailed direction so that it is both aggregated and detailed.

To understand the impact of proper S&OP, one must think long-term. The following quotation provides explanation as to what types of decisions are made in which planning horizon.

> *"The immediate, short, medium, long and very long time frame forecasts should be tied to specific resource decisions. The immediate time frame forecast should be the basis for material changes and the schedule changes. These decisions are reactions to specific changes in demand forecast. The short decision time frame is used to make specific changes in the number of workers. The medium decision time frame is used for making equipment changes (purchase or disposal). The decision to bring in new equipment is based on meeting competitive objectives. The long-term decision time frame is used for substantial changes in technology."*
> – Sales Forecasting for Strategic Resource Planning

Two of the most important aspects of any planning process is its planning horizon (how far into the future that the plan 'sees') and the planning interval (how frequently the planning process is performed). S&OP is generally performed as a **monthly process** and therefore is an infrequent type of planning. Unlike more frequent types of planning, S&OP tends not to be done by individuals that only perform S&OP. The executives that participate in S&OP are busy doing other things for most of the month, and then come together monthly in a series of meetings to participate in S&OP. The time features of S&OP are the following:

1. *Planning Horizon:* Between 1 to 5 years, with 1 to 2 years being the most commonly cited in the literature on S&OP.

2. *Planning Frequency or Interval:* Monthly

3. *Planning Bucket:* Monthly (this is how the data is aggregated in terms of the planning periods within the planning horizon)

The Structure of the Book

This book will address multiple areas of S&OP, which will include a general background survey of the history of S&OP, the relationship between S&OP and IBP, S&OP methods, and the pitfalls in establishing an effective process. Applications including SAP IBP, Anaplan, SAP Cash Management and Demand Works Smoothie are covered to show how S&OP and financial planning are performed in software.

The S&OP Software Category

S&OP is a category of software that has, within the past few years, begun to see significant software development, despite the fact that the term was first coined back in the 1980s and the process has been used by corporations, large and small, for decades. Even now, the vast majority of S&OP "systems" are worked out in spreadsheets and, interestingly, most of the S&OP applications either look like spreadsheets or have areas that allow porting out to a spreadsheet. S&OP systems have, for the most part, relied upon the output from other applications: supply planning, demand planning, and production planning systems, for example. Data from these other tools are often imported and then converted to a financial analysis to be fed to an S&OP system. Some vendors have now introduced functionality where the planning processing is performed in the S&OP system rather than in the systems that traditionally fed S&OP systems with output.

Books and Other Publications on S&OP

As with all my books, I performed a comprehensive literature review before I began writing. One of my favorite quotations about research is from the highly respected RAND Corporation, a "think tank" based in sunny Santa Monica, CA. They are located not far from where I grew up. On my lost surfing weekends during high school, I used to walk right by their offices with my friend — at that time having no idea of the institution's historical significance. RAND's *Standards for High Quality Research and Analysis* publication makes the following statement about how its research references other work.

> *"A high-quality study cannot be done in intellectual isolation: it necessarily builds on and contributes to a body of research and analysis. The relationships between a given study and its predecessors should be rich and explicit. The study team's understanding of past research should be evident in many aspects of its work, from the way in which the problem is formulated and approached to the discussion of the findings and their implications. The team should take particular care to explain the ways in which its study agrees, disagrees, or otherwise differs importantly from previous studies. Failure to demonstrate an understanding of previous research lowers the perceived quality of a study, despite any other good characteristics it may possess."*

S&OP is a strategic subject and has, thus, generated many "Pollyanna-ish" books and articles which provide a sunny interpretation of the challenges that face S&OP. In many publications, S&OP is presented as very close to a miracle cure that will solve almost all the coordination problems within a company. I have been in countless meetings or interviews where the person seated across from me wistfully opined, "If only we had a real S&OP process..."

The best-known books on S&OP are the series by Thomas F. Wallace, who, although not the "inventor" of S&OP, probably did the most to publicize the concept and make it broadly known. These books helped start the TF Wallace consulting company, and these are the most common books on S&OP that I often found distributed out at my clients. It's hard to disagree with most of what is written in these books as they are logical and straightforward affairs.

These books never claimed to provide the details of constructing the systems and support structure for S&OP, and S&OP is one of the least standardized and disciplined of all the planning processes within companies. There are several books on S&OP but I don't feel compelled to mention them because they tend to make a lot of large claims, but don't really explain how to overcome the common problems in setting up an S&OP process. For many years, there really were no S&OP applications worth mentioning, but setting up an effective S&OP process is extremely tricky, and some of the books in this area don't seem to acknowledge that. I will get into all of these issues in this book, and provide a realistic appraisal of the challenges.

In addition to books on S&OP there is also a book on integrated business planning or IBP. Its title is *Transition from Sales and Operations Planning to Integrated Business Planning*. It is very similar in orientation to the books on S&OP that I have described above. None of the books on S&OP or IBP focus on systems, which is where this books differs quite dramatically. This book is very much about getting S&OP systems to work properly to support the S&OP process, and ensuring a consistency between S&OP software and the systems used to plan for changing demand, the manage supply chains and to organize production.

The S&OP process is a collaborative one that has many similarities with other types of collaborative forecasting and planning. It is anything but easy. A good example of this is collaborative sales forecasting, which is described well by the following quotation.

> *"Anyone in sales understands the time-tested ritual of the Monday morning sales call. Typically, the call goes smoothly and everyone is excited about the week ahead, the progress being made at key accounts, and the promise of closing several significant deals. Then suddenly those dreaded words are spoken, 'Forecasts are due this Friday" triggering a collective sigh from attendees on the call. The energy built in the first 58 minutes of the call is quickly deflated in the final 2. While we all understand that updating forecasts is an important process on the road to hitting company revenue targets, it can be one of those exercises that most would readily admit they*

*would rather not undertake. Forecasting is not met with such
disdain because of what it is, but because of how it is done. The
painstaking process of collecting updates from reps spread out across
the country or the globe; consolidating forecasts into a single report
that sales executives, finance executives, and others can understand;
and communicating changes and how they have an impact on the
company's revenue targets is not for the faint of heart. Most often
the sales forecast, once compiled, is already out of date and not very
useful for the intended stakeholders."*

— Misery to Mastery

The best way to be successful with S&OP is to have a realistic understanding of the challenges in S&OP from all the perspectives, technological, political, etc.

S&OP Software Overview

As with any enterprise software category, there are many vendors that claim to have an S&OP application, but most don't really have an S&OP application. In fact there are few "true" S&OP applications at the time of this book's publishing and, consequently, S&OP software is still a small software category despite its popularity as a topic of discussion. The reason for the delay is that the S&OP process is considerably more complex than, say, demand planning, requiring many different inputs and significant subjective elements. This conspires to make development trickier. Perhaps because of this higher complexity, many companies have not shown the same interest in spending money on S&OP applications as they have on other software categories. The good news, however, is that there've been numerous positive developments in the last few years, and I've had the privilege to review many of your options for true S&OP applications. The only downside is that, as the software gains in complexity, the learning curve associated with it comes steeper, and it will require more maintenance. Most companies haven't yet begun to realize that there will be a need for dedicated S&OP managers and maintenance groups in the future, which is a matter of some concern.

The best-known software vendor in the S&OP space is Steelwedge, but many other vendors are actively working on improving their S&OP applications. SAP is on its fourth S&OP product with SAP IBP, which is showcased in this book. S&OP applications are interesting in that many of them do not have their own user interface as much as they are plug-ins to Excel, and most of the S&OP applications borrow very heavily from the spreadsheet motif. This book shows screenshots from both supply chain planning systems and S&OP applications. This is consistent with the approach in other SCM Focus Press books in that multiple applications are used to demonstrate principles of the topic area. The author is not aligned with any particular software. This is a positive for readers, as books by people that work for software vendors or who are aligned to a software vendor tend to result in positively biased coverage of the application.

Why Forecasting Software is Only One Part of an S&OP Analysis

Whether experts in S&OP like it or not, the S&OP process has become overwhelmingly associated with forecasting. But, a complete S&OP process means going beyond forecasting, it means having a mechanism for understanding the **benefits** along with the **cost** of increasing **capacity**.

Budgeting is the ability to pay for things that are required to meet the consensus sales forecast, such as inventory; it also happens to be the main focal point in most discussions about S&OP. However, a second important part of the funding question is the capital improvements that can be required to meet the consensus forecast. Capital improvements are an example of constraints, which can be changed, and are much more complicated to estimate than the effect of carrying different levels of inventory. The more stable the business, the more straightforward budgeting will be. However, some decisions, such as funding highly expensive chip fabrication plants, require quite a lot of financial analysis. Tesla's Gigafactory, a giant lithium-ion battery factory in Nevada, broke ground in 2014, and will not be finished until 2017. It had a $5 billion project cost (shared by Tesla, Panasonic and the State of Nevada). It will employ 6500 people and will supply 500,000 cars per year (in addition to other battery uses). This is based upon a forecast of a much higher future demand of this battery technology. This is where very serious S&OP is necessary– such forecasts should be the subject of intense scrutiny.

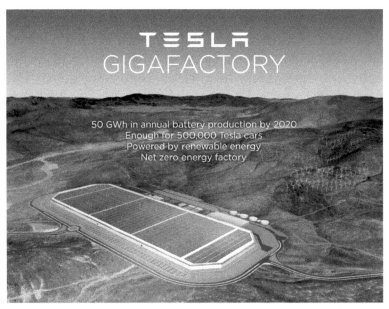

One wonders what the S&OP meetings for the Gigafactory – which involved two private companies (at the very least) and the state of Nevada – must have looked like. The State of Nevada, has to perform its own S&OP process as it estimated a $100 billion of economic activity for the State of Nevada over a 20 year period, promoting it to offer $1.25 million in incentives in order to secure the Tesla/Panasonic project in Nevada versus a competing state.

The Use of Screen Shots in the Book

I consult in some popular and well-known applications, and I've found that companies have often been given the wrong impression of an application's capabilities. As part of my consulting work, I am required to present the results of testing various applications. The research may show that a well-known application is not able to perform some functionality well enough to be used by a company, and point to a lesser-known application where this functionality is easily performed. Because I am routinely in this situation, I am asked to provide evidence of the testing results within applications, and screen shots provide this necessary evidence.

Furthermore, some time ago, it became a habit for me to include extensive screen shots in most of my project documentation. A screen shot does not, of course, guarantee that a particular functionality works, but it is the best that can be done in a document format. Everything in this book exists in one application or another, and nothing described in this book is hypothetical.

Timing Field Definitions Identification

This book is filled with lists. Some of these lists are field definitions. The way to quickly identify which lists are field definitions, they will be all *italics*, while lists that are not field definitions will be only *italics* for the term defined, while the definition that follows is in normal text.

How Writing Bias Is Controlled at SCM Focus and SCM Focus Press

Bias is a serious problem in the enterprise software field. Large vendors receive uncritical coverage of their products, and large consulting companies recommend the large vendors that have the resources to hire and pay consultants rather than the vendors with the best software for the client's needs.

At SCM Focus, we have yet to financially benefit from a company's decision to buy an application showcased in print, either in a book or on the SCM Focus website. This may change in the future as SCM Focus grows – but we have been writing with a strong viewpoint for years without coming into any conflicts of interest. SCM Focus has the most stringent rules related to controlling bias and restricting commercial influence of any information provider. These "writing rules" are provided in the link below:

   http://www.scmfocus.com/writing-rules/

If other information providers followed these rules, we would be able to learn about software without being required to perform our own research and testing for every topic.

Information about enterprise supply chain planning software can be found on the Internet, but this information is primarily promotional or written at such a high level that none of the important details or limitations of the application are exposed; this is true of books as well. When only one enterprise software application is covered in a book, one will find that the application works perfectly; the application operates as expected and there are no problems during the implementation to bring the application live. This is all quite amazing and quite different from my experience of implementing enterprise software. However, it is very difficult to make a living by providing objective information about enterprise supply chain software, especially as it means being critical at some point. I once remarked to a friend that SCM Focus had very little competition in providing untarnished information on this software category, and he said, "Of course, there is no money in it."

The Approach to the Book

By writing this book, I wanted to help people get exactly the information they need without having to read a lengthy volume. The approach to the book is essentially the same as to my previous books, and in writing this book I followed the same principles.

1. **Be direct and concise.** There is very little theory in this book and the math that I cover is simple. While the mathematics behind the optimization methods for supply and production planning is involved, there are plenty of books, which cover this topic. This book is focused on software and for most users and implementers of the software the most important thing to understand is conceptually what the software is doing.

2. **Based on project experience.** Nothing in the book is hypothetical; I have worked with it or tested it on an actual project. My project experience has led to my understanding a number of things that are not covered in typical supply planning books. In this book, I pass on this understanding to you.

3. **Saturate the book with graphics.** Roughly two-thirds of a human's sensory input is visual,and books that do not use graphics—especially educational and training books such as this one—can fall short of their purpose. Graphics have also been used consistently and extensively on the SCM Focus website.

Important Terminology

This book will use a variety of terminology that it is necessary to know in order to understand the book. These terms are divided into different categories.

The SCM Focus Site

As I am also the author of the SCM Focus site, http://www.scmfocus.com, the site and the book share a number of concepts and graphics. Furthermore, this book contains many links to articles on the site, which provide more detail on specific subjects. This book provides an explanation of how supply and production planning software works and aims to continue to be a reference after its initial reading. However, if your interest in supply planning software continues to grow, the SCM Focus site is a good resource to which articles are continually added.

CHAPTER 2

The Relationship Between Planning Systems and S&OP Systems

How planning systems and S&OP interact is an important question because it is not well covered in S&OP publications. As I pointed out in the introduction, none of the books written up to the point of this book's publication have focused on the available S&OP systems, and most articles have little from the systems perspective. Instead, publications on S&OP have tended to be written from the perspective of strategies and theory. In fact, the vast majority of consulting in S&OP tends to be from the strategy side. Therefore, the systems' details are going to tend to be overlooked. Once one delves into the details of using S&OP applications, alongside external planning systems, many issues that must be resolved become apparent. Later in this book, when we discuss SAP IBP, Anaplan and SAP Cash Management, we raise questions as to the level of planning detail needed within SAP IBP and Anaplan, as some of the detail that I will show is actually **a duplicate** of the supply chain planning that is performed in a system like SAP APO. We will begin this chapter by describing the normal relationship between planning systems and S&OP systems, before describing how new S&OP applications like SAP IBP and Anaplan have changed that traditional relationship.

Services S&OP

This book focuses on S&OP for companies with a supply chain, either manufacturers or distributors, since this is where most of the S&OP-related focus lies. One of the interesting aspects of writing this book was searching for material on S&OP in the services sector and seeing how little there was to read. However, S&OP is a universal process, as every entity must balance supply and demand. For whatever reason, S&OP receives light coverage with respect to service industries.

If we consider a bank, it's clear that the same issues of balancing supply and demand that would apply to a manufacturing company, also apply to S&OP. In fact, given how phone support customer service quality has declined over the past several decades, and how wait times have dramatically increased, (one of the favorite messages which plays on support lines is *"we are facing abnormally high call volumes, thank your for your patience"*). In addition to outsourcing phone support to very low cost countries that have lower quality English skills, one might ask how good a job service companies are doing with respect to their S&OP processes as they have clearly cut quality, costs and capacity – but have generally not reduced the prices for insurance, banking, etc. These are some of the most elementary types of planning and yet they are beyond so many companies that can't see past cutting costs and fail to realize that they may be hurting their sales. The relationship between investment and sales and profit is what S&OP is all about. Here, we see how disconnected executives have become from the central issue in S&OP

> *"In fact 90% of executives see Customer Service as crucial to their future business success. In the same study more than 70% of senior call center executives revealed that their companies fail to meet their customers' expectations, according to Bain. So we have a strange dichotomy. Organizations know that good customer service is essential to their future success; they understand that there is a real tangible cost and risk of dissatisfied customers defecting and yet these same organizations seem incapable of affecting change."*
> – Why is Most Call Center Service so Bad?

This performance is mirrored in the customer's perception. According to Lee

Resources, while 80% of companies think they deliver superior service, only 8% of their customers think the same thing.

This brings up the topic of how companies understand the value produced by their call centers.

> *"In fact, for many organizations it is the primary communications channel and the only meaningful one that facilitates a two way discussion, a dialogue. Failing to recognize this fact leads organizations to undervalue the contribution the call center and broader customer service and technical support plays in sustaining the business. Not only can a call center generate revenue through orders, up-sell and extensions, but the call center also protects revenue already promised through solving issues and fixing problems, many of which were not caused or created by the call center."*
>
> – Why is Most Call Center Service so Bad?

This is a misunderstanding of how service affects the company's bottom line. Companies that score the worst in call center customer service, companies like Citibank, American Airlines, Comcast, Blue Cross Blue Shield, Bank of America, etc have big advertising budgets, but don't put the money they need to into call centers. Are these companies that understand the relationship between investing in their service capacity and their bottom line?

A certain number of customers will call on the phone to a call center or walk through any bank door, or ask for a number of services with which the employees must be fully versed, and the bank must balance demand and supply. Therefore, they must, in some way, perform a high-level match between supply and demand, and find a way to fund this – that is, they must engage in some form of S&OP process. Booz Allen Hamilton wrote a paper that covers S&OP specifically in the financial services industry and brought up the following questions faced by financial services companies.

- "How much call waiting time should be allowed for different customer segments?

- How long should the queues in our branches be allowed to grow?

- How short should our account processing lead-time be?

- How long should it take for our new customers to open an account, or buy a policy from us?

- How accurate should our response rates be?

- How should we prioritize new product introductions?

- What type of flexibility should we build into our operational capacity, taking into account the cost/service trade off?"

Therefore, I wanted to establish that services S&OP is just as important as S&OP for manufacturers and distributors.

For purely service companies, S&OP applications must be integrated with different types of software that are specific to their needs, a good example of this being call center software. Software like TalkDesk or ZenDesk, records the timing and duration of calls, and create a database that can be used as the basis for further analyses. This create a usage history, which can then be correlated with the sales forecast to predict how many more resources will be required to service different types of calls. Overall, the question of adding supply is much simpler than in manufacturing, as the capacity normally comes down to adding or subtracting people or adjusting the systems that these people use. I will now continue discussing the implication of supply chain planning systems with S&OP, fully cognizant that services S&OP would not use a supply chain planning system.

The Traditional Interaction between S&OP and Planning Systems

Traditionally, the S&OP system is fed by the output of supply chain planning systems combined with financial data, which includes the price and the cost of the item. For the vast majority of companies, at the time of this book's publishing, they still perform S&OP without the use of an application, and instead with spreadsheets. Unless they put a high degree of effort into creating a very detailed S&OP spreadsheet and updating it with information regarding constraints, the company will **not** have the ability to do much more than incorporate the final forecast with the final supply plan and to dollarize the resulting inventory position. Therefore the following are often what is sent to S&OP systems from either an external planning system or the ERP system.

1. The Forecast

2. The Supply Plan

3. Costs and Prices

Costs and prices allow the dollarization of the sales and operations plan, and costs allow for things like inventory costs to be calculated, while the inclusion of prices allows profitability to be calculated.

We can look at an application that represents this type of S&OP, although it is both a demand and supply planning system as well as an S&OP system. This application is called Demand Works Smoothie.

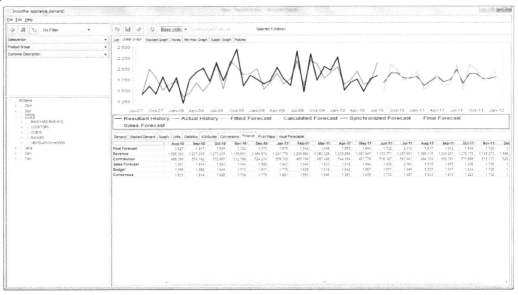

In Demand Works Smoothie, one can see the dollarization of the forecast.

Forecast adjustment is used to perform simulation. If demand increased by different amounts what would be the effect on the system? This forecast adjustment should not be confused with the actual forecast, which has been determined through extensive demand planning and sales forecasting.

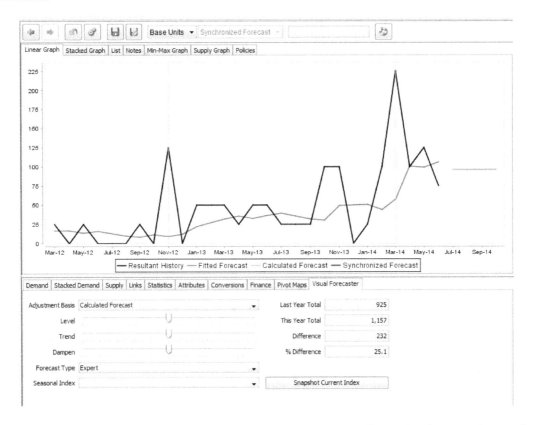

Demand Works Smoothie has one of the easiest ways to adjust the forecast.It employs sliders. Here we begin with the sliders in a neutral state.

S&OP is performed at a high level of aggregation. Therefore, when a change is made it is necessary that the change be applied to a grouping, rather than having to make the change to each product location combination at a time – which would be impossible in an S&OP setting. In fact any application that is used for S&OP must be very effective at grouping products and geographies. This is discussed in more detail in Chapter 6: S&OP, Aggregation and Forecast Hierarchies.

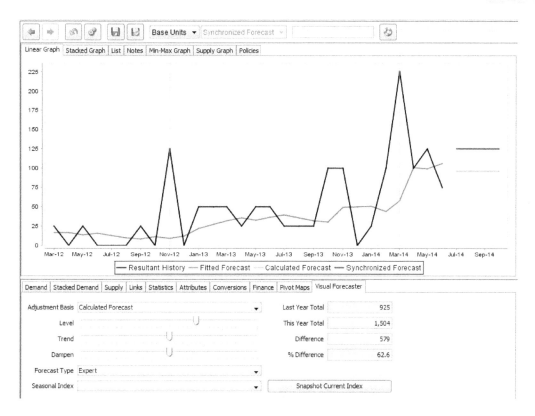

*This shows the **level** of the forecast brought up. So the forecast is now higher by the percentage that I moved the slider. This adjustment using the sliders can be performed at any level of the hierarchy, from a single SKU to all of the products and all of the locations in one fell swoop. After the forecast has been adjusted, Smoothie can run the supply plan.*

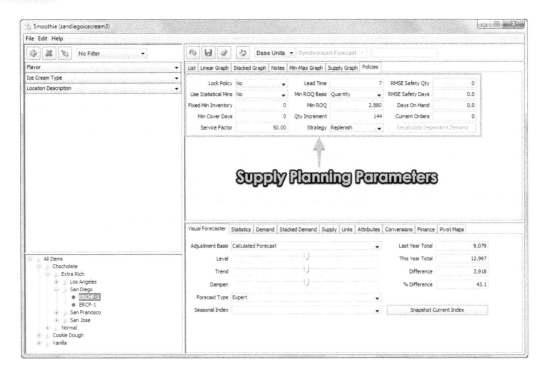

The same aggregation functionality that was shown in the previous forecast adjust-ment screen shot is also useful for supply planning. These are the supply planning parameters. They control the supply plan, and they can be changed for any grouping that is selected. For instance a minimum number of coverage days (which controls inventory level) could be set for either the entire product database or for only parts of the product database. A company could simulate the changes brought about by paying more to suppliers which would allow the specific component's lead time to decline, de-creasing the lead time for the overall finished good. This could be done by selecting only the components for which the program is applicable and changing the lead-time for all of them, and then recalculating the supply plan.

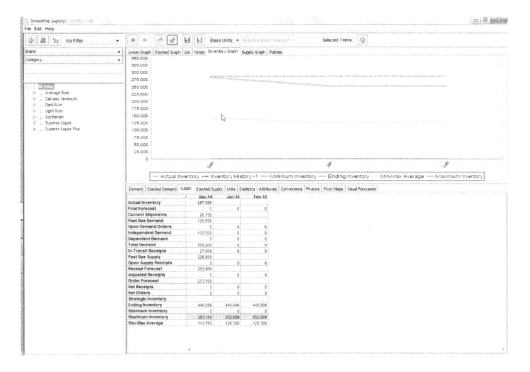

This view shows the supply plan. The supply plan can be run very easily off of the menu.

Because S&OP is integrated into Smoothie, any change made to the demand plan and supply plan is **immediately shown** in the S&OP tab of the application, greatly reducing the complexity of integrating a separate S&OP system to the demand and supply planning system. This is an important distinction that it can be difficult to get across to executive decision makers during a demo. One caveat is that Smoothie does not deal with production beyond the application of the production lot size that can be added to Smoothie's master data parameters. Smoothie is not a production planning system, and therefore Smoothie does not deal with manufacturing resources. This means, as with other systems which are similarly designed, that there is no restriction or even any visibility to the scheduling of overcapacity.

What we've just shown is the most common approach to S&OP in systems in terms of what is modeled, except that, in Smoothie, demand, supply and S&OP planning are all done from within one application. When the demand and supply planning systems and S&OP are all separate from one another, this requires integration, increases the time lag, and reduces the ability of the S&OP application to be rerun without becoming out of synch with the demand and supply planning systems.

This approach is not comprehensive, however, it provides a system with a reasonable overhead. It also prevents the executives from making many adjustments to the demand, supply or production plan. I will explain further on why this is a good thing. Now we will move on to the more advanced S&OP applications.

The More Advanced Approach to S&OP

Please note, I didn't title this subsection "a better approach" since it is far from clear that advanced approaches produce better results in the real world. That being said, the more advanced approach has the S&OP application incorporating some of the master data from existing planning systems and producing its own plans, rather than merely parroting back the preliminary supply and demand plans done in isolation. Under this design, the following information is sent to the S&OP system. The bold items are new or net change from the previous list.

1. The Forecast

2. **Sales history**

3. Costs and Prices

4. The Supply Plan

5. **Capacities** (sent from the supply planning/production planning system, includes things like resource capacity, downtime, resource availability times per day, etc..)

6. **Lot Sizing** (sent from the supply planning/production planning system.)

7. **Reorder Points** (sent from the supply planning/production planning system.)

SAP IBP includes the ability of SAP to generate a **statistical forecast** (as opposed to simply receiving a forecast from the external forecasting system).

It also has the ability to **run heuristics** that produce a supply and production plan, rather than simply representing the supply/production plan from elsewhere. In Chapter 4:SAP IBP, ANAPLAN & SAP Cash Management, I will get into more detail on SAP IBP and the implications of such detail and complexity.

A Standard S&OP Process

If we look at a standard S&OP process, it looks something like the following:

1. *Review and Sign Off on the Demand Plan:* It all begins with demand. Therefore, in order to progress through the S&OP process, this first step must be accomplished.

2. *Review and Sign Off on the Supply Plan*: The supply plan contains both the inventory that will need to be brought into the supply network and the production that is to be performed by the company (in the case where the company in question is a manufacturer).

3. *Review and Sign Off on the Financial Plan*: The financial plan is dependent upon the finalization of the supply plan.

Review and Sign Off on the Demand Plan

It should first be pointed out that, in terms of **normal supply chain planning**, not all companies actually **need** to forecast demand for their products in order to run their business. For example, defense contractors frequently know years in advance what they will be building because they have firm government contracts that contain quantities and dates. This is called a **build to order** or **make to order** manufacturing environment.[1]

Defense contractors receive their sales orders so far out that the sales order simply takes the place of a forecast. And the sales orders are further out than

---

[1] An important feature of the various manufacturing environments is that the **relationship** between the demand signal and the beginning of production orprocurement is not always the same for all of the products in the BOM or recipe.Manufacturing environments are covered in the SCM Focus Press book, *Replenishment Triggers: Setting Systems for Make to Stock, Make to Order & Assemble to Order.*

the combined lead-time for both procurement and manufacturing. This greatly improves the ability to plan as the supply plan can be based on a known quantity rather than a forecast, which will always have some degree of error. The S&OP process for a build to order company is, as such, much simpler. It means that the sales plan (rather than the demand plan) is confirmed quickly, and the company can move quickly into supply plan confirmation. The manufacturing environments that are available to a company have less to do with what the company "wants to do," and more to do with the particular product the company produces combined with the type of market into which the product is sold. So while most companies would, if they had the option, prefer to be "make to order" environments to reduce supply chain complexity and costs, in reality, most companies must follow the make to stock manufacturing strategy because their procurement and manufacturing lead times are longer than the customer is willing to wait. However, in terms of S&OP, **all companies, make to order, assemble to order and make to stock alike** need to develop a financial forecast – not for supply chain planning but to **determine how to setup and constrain the business**. Make to order businesses may (if the sales orders are far enough out) use the sales orders as the "forecasts" for the S&OP process. However, most companies are not make to order, and therefore most companies do need to produce a **supply chain forecast**. This means that a forecast will almost always precede the forecast that is produced/adjusted in the S&OP process.

How Many Forecasts?

Within companies often the term "the forecast" is used. As in "the forecast is not accurate." However, any company conducting a proper planning strategy will have multiple forecasts. There is a sales forecast, a supply chain forecast, a marketing forecast, and so on. All of these must be coalesced into a single forecast for S&OP. The final forecast exists outside of the S&OP system. That is to say, a final forecast must be generated **whether or not an S&OP process exists**.

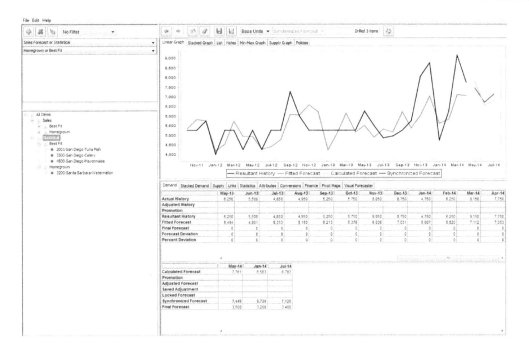

In Demand Works Smoothie, which is primarily a supply planning system, notice the row titled "Final Forecast" in the screen shot above. Most demand planning systems have a row, which represents the final forecast.

Review and Sign off on the Supply Plan

After the demand plan is agreed to, the supply plan review and sign off can begin. A supply plan (which contains, within it, the production plan), in a make to stock and assemble to order environment – where a forecast is produced either at the finished good or at the assembly level – means triggering supply. Replenishment triggers are actions that cause replenishment to occur. The term replenishment is easy to comingle in one's mind with purchasing. However, the replenishment strategy drives both procured materials and produced materials. To replenish simply means **to fill again**. But when we speak about replenishment, we're not just discussing the inventory to be sold, we're also talking about the raw materials needed to produce the inventory and support its manufacturing. A replenishment trigger can be either demand-based (from a forecast or a sales order falling into a particular planning bucket) or supply-based, in the form of a reorder point (a level of stock or raw material at which point a re-supply order is triggered).

Supply and production planning systems can be capacity constrained. Constraint-based planning works by setting up resources, anything from factory equipment to transportation units to handling equipment, in the model. Resources are then assigned limitations in capacity and/or availability (e.g., they have a specific capacity and can only be run from 8 a.m. to 10 p.m.).

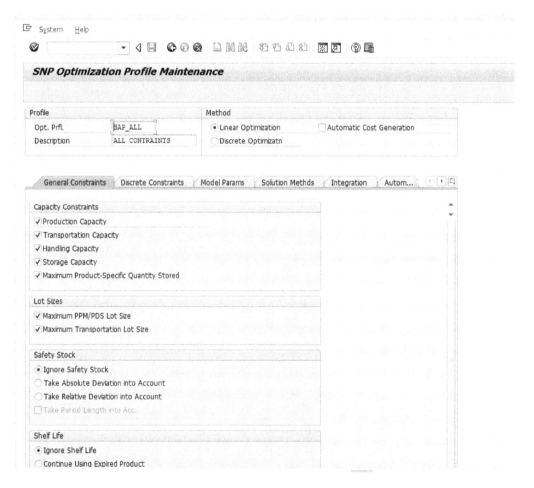

*In SAP APO, the supply-planning module, called SNP, can constrain on different types of resources. A constraint is something that restricts the capacity of the system. Supply and production planning systems that can constrain, allow resources to be constrained or unconstrained, that is not all resources that are setup in a these systems is necessarily constrained. All of this allows the application to create a "feasible plan" which means that the application will **not attempt to meet demand in a way that exceeds the capacity of the system**.*

Constraining is the more sophisticated way of producing a supply and production plan. The other way is to perform capacity leveling.[2] Constraining a resources also allows for more effective multi-level planning, and constraint based planning means less manual work in capacity leveling, but it also requires a more sophisticated set of a capabilities in the implementing company and more investment into setting up the system.

Capacity Leveling

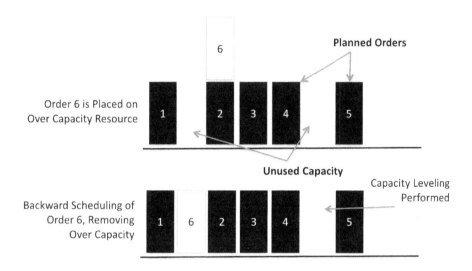

In capacity leveling, the leveling is performed either by a procedure or manually. The top portion of the graphic is after the initial or network supply planning run. This

---

[2] With unconstrained planning (or infinite planning), capacities may or may not be declared—and, if they are declared, there is nothing to stop the system from placing an unlimited load on any resource. A second planning pass called the capacity-leveling run must then adjust this. This topic is referred to as capacity planning. The details behind the differences between constraint based planning and capacity leveling are very important, particularly with respect to how capacity is managed at various levels of the bill of material. If you'd like to learn more about constraints on supply chain planning, we recommend you follow up with the SCM Focus Press book: *Constrained Supply and Production Planning in SAP APO*.

All of this has important implications for performing capacity planning in the S&OP system as systems like SAP IBP, that is S&OP systems that perform capacity management within the application.

*places the demand upon the resource based upon the need date, which is in turn based upon the need date (minus the lead times). When capacity is not constrained, there is no consideration given to what is feasible. Then, the capacity leveling process moves the planned production order from periods, which are **over capacity** to periods, which have **capacity**. The lower portion of the graphic above is after capacity leveling has been performed.[3]*

Both of these approaches move the demand forward or backward along the planning time horizon. Scheduling can be performed in two directions, but there are more than two options because the directions can be combined in one scheduling setting. How far forward or backward scheduling is performed is controlled in the settings.

1. *Forward Scheduling:* For the start date, the system uses the beginning of the period in which the production quantities were entered. From this start date, the system calculates in a forward direction to determine the finish date. The system displays the order quantities on the production start date.

2. *Backward Scheduling:* For the finish date, the system uses the end of the period in which the production quantities were entered. From this finish date, the system calculates in a backward direction to determine the start date.

3. *Backward / Forward Scheduling:* Here the system works in two steps:

   a. In the first step, the system uses the end of the period in which the production quantities were entered as the finish date. From this finish date, the system calculates in a backward direction to determine the start date.

   b. In the second step, the system uses the beginning of the period cal-

---

[3] Capacity leveling cannot necessarily be performed for every resource in a system. Capacity leveling only works in SNP for production resources and transportation resources, **and does not work for storage or handling resources**. In SAP APO capacity leveling only works on four of the resource types: bucket, single-mixed, multi-mixed, and transportation. Furthermore, SNP capacity leveling only takes into account SNP planned orders and SNP stock transfers. Different application manage capacity leveling in different ways per resource type.

culated in step one and then schedules forwards. Order processing commences at the beginning of the start period calculated by the system and ends in the period specified by the planner.

Furthermore, different supply planning methods allow for different scheduling to be performed, and scheduling direction has different implications depending up the supply planning method that is selected. This requires that the resources be setup in the system and that the resources be updated so that they more or less reflect the actual capacity of the resources available to the company.

Generally, only the **production** resources are actually constrained within a company even though some systems allow for more than production resources to be technically constrained. Unlike production resources, supply-planning resources (storage, location, shipping and receiving, and transportation) are **not in a** sequential line. When each is used, the supply planning resources have substantial lags between them, and they are also much more flexible in that they are less prone to absolute constraints, and as such, while constraint based supply planning systems were copied in their approach from production planning systems, the model of constraints never worked as well for supply planning resources (storage, location, shipping resources, etc..) Clearly, the production planning constraining requirement is a much easier one to meet than the requirement of constraining supply planning resources. Therefore, the most common resources to be constrained in supply planning systems are not supply planning resources, but production resources, although they are of less detail than the same production resources that are entered into the production planning system. There is a lot more detail around this topic, which goes beyond the scope of this book. To read more about finite and bottleneck resources see this post below:

http://www.scmfocus.com/sapplanning/2009/07/01/bottleneck-resources/

To read more about the types of resources that are included in supply planning systems see this post below:

http://www.scmfocus.com/supplyplanning/2011/10/02/commonly-used-and-unused-constraints-for-supply-planning/

Having provided some coverage to resources conceptually and how they different in supply and production planning systems, let us dive into a supply planning system to review resources.

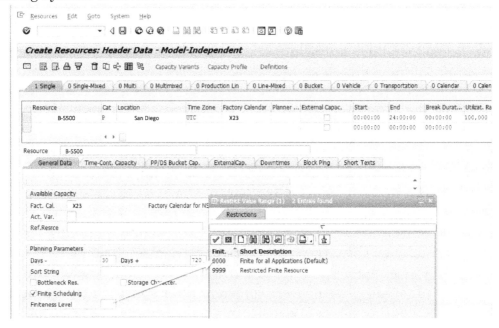

This is the view of a resource in SAP SNP. The resource has a defined capacity, which includes how long the resource can be operated per day, its capacity when operated, etc.

In some S&OP systems, the resource data, as with the example provided previously with Demand Works Smoothie, is not copied over from either the ERP system or the external planning system. Not all companies employ **external supply chain planning systems** and those that don't tend to rely very heavily on spreadsheets as planning within ERP systems which is normally quite limiting.

Resources get a huge amount of attention in supply and production planning; however, the resource is only one of the types of constraints that are modeled by a supply chain planning system. Therefore, if the plan is not simply sent from the supply chain planning system to the S&OP system, it would need to similarly be **modeled** in the S&OP system. Another constraint is the production order batch or lot sizes. This is the minimum quantity in which a material is either procured or produced. Production lot sizes simply declare the batch in which an order must be produced (500 units, 1000 units, etc.) without declaring whether or not that lot size quantity is feasible, or if there is any capacity to produce that item requested by the supply planning system. For example, a production order may be created for 500 units on a specific day, but in actual fact, the resource is not available to produce 500 units on that day because it is out for maintenance. Another example of a constraint is the factory calendar, which determines **when** the factory can accept capacity.

The traditional output of a supply planning system is planned production orders— purchase requisitions and stock transfer requisitions. Planned production orders and purchase requisitions are created by the initial/network supply planning run, and stock transfer requisitions are created by the deployment run.

Deployment Plan

After the initial or network supply plan is generated, a second process, referred to as the deployment plan, is necessary. While the initial or network supply plan brings material into the supply network and schedules production orders, the **deployment plan moves the material through the supply network and out to customers**. This deployment plan is generated within the supply planning application.

Now that we have discussed finalizing the demand and supply plan, we can move to the financial plan.

Review and Sign off on the Financial Plan

The financial plan is a dependent entity based upon the supply (and production) plan. For manufacturing and distribution companies, the first obvious financial implication is inventory. When a specific average inventory position is calculated, it means a **specific allocation of capital in order to fund that inventory level.** The normal overhead costs are included which includes the office overhead, along with factory overhead, etc. Overhead of existing expenditures is already known by finance before arriving at an S&OP meeting, so finance is looking for the costs of things that are dependent upon the supply plan. Finance will have funded the company up to the present point, and therefore is looking for net change costs. The S&OP planning process is one of the few planning processes within a company where the constraints can be questioned and changed. Therefore, while other planning processes are about working within the existing constraints, S&OP is very much about **challenging the existing constraints**. If we can take a specific example, when there is too much demand for a particular period, supply chain planning tries to backwards or forward schedule the demand on the existing resource. However, in S&OP, if the plan shows long-term overcapacity, the S&OP process is to determine if it makes financial sense to add capacity. And in fact, this brings up an important point -- that it is unlikely that the executives will be able to redo the work of managing demand within the existing constraints better than the planners -- the primary value of the S&OP process is in changing the existing constraints or in evaluating if the existing constraints are worth changing.

Global Versus Regional S&OP

Although not frequently discussed as one would think, a big part of S&OP is at what geographic level it is performed. Various S&OP processes at different hierarchies in geography can mean including the S&OP process below it. This also means that there are **multiple** S&OP meetings throughout the month, and that the higher S&OP meetings are dependent upon the meeting outcomes below them. In fact, for larger companies in particular, it can be quite a bit of work just scheduling all of the meeting and managing the flow of plans from the regional up to the national then global S&OP processes. Each meeting has an assigned group of individuals. Some companies create a matrix, which lays out which individuals are assigned to which groups. Ultimately, one person should own each of the meetings, which is the same person that has the ultimate final approval for the S&OP plan for that particular area. One of the issues with S&OP that reduces its buy-in is that many S&OP meetings end up being rehashes of information that was discussed in other forums, and the moderator is unwilling to enforce the meeting topic to be constrained to the S&OP topics specifically.

Country Plan				Global Plan		
1.	Country Plan Summary	View product level country plan vs. global target		6.	Global Target Summary	- View yearly sales and profit targets - Compare growth % by country
2.	Price Input	Configure sales price increase at category and brand level View YoY sales price growth		7.	Sales Target Set	Define yearly global sales targets
3.	Volume Input	- Set volume growth on market assumptions - Run market growth and share scenarios		8.	Net Sales Summary	Analyze yearly sales growth by geo Compare product yearly sales targets
4.	Brand Positioning Summary	Examine products position within the market		9.	Target Allocation by Brand & Innovation	- Define target allocation by brand - Measure incremental sales from new product innovation
5.	Advertising & Promotion Input	Create A&P cost assumptions based on market position		10.	Target Allocation by Country	- View target allocation by geo based on historical YoY growth
				11.	Profit Margin Target Set	- Define yearly PBO margin targets

Here we can see Anaplan allows the individual to go right into the area that is applicable. After changes have been made at the regional level, they roll up to the levels above this automatically.

Timing When to Expand Capacity

Within the discussion of capacity planning and adding capacity with capital improvements, the question of timing is always important. The company does not want to add capacity too soon – and risk not being able to use the capacity, or having to repurpose the capacity, and does not want to add capacity too late, as it will miss out on market opportunities and therefore profits. If we think outside of manufacturing and distribution for a moment, real estate is a perfect example of this conundrum. Economic cycles are difficult to predict, but building must be planned years in advance of the anticipated opening date. Many large-scale hotels were greenlit to be built right before the great recession of 2007-2008. The recession hit as several hotels were being built, and they suffered from low occupancy for years as Las Vegas tourist volumes too quite some time to recover. Clearly, many of those hotels would have never been built if the backers had a crystal ball.

> *"The timing variable in a capacity strategy is concerned with the balance between the forecasted demand for capacity and the supply of capacity. If there is a capacity demand surplus the utilization will be high, thus enabling a low cost profile, but there is also a risk of losing customers due to long delivery lead times. A capacity supply surplus on the other hand creates a higher cost profile by due to surplus capacity it is easier to maintain high delivery reliability and*

flexibility. The capacity strategy can thus be expressed as a tradeoff between high utilization and maintaining a capacity cushion."
– Linking the Perspectives from Manufacturing Strategy and
Sales Operations Planning

A company can choose when to expand capacity and can be aggressive or less aggressive. This tradeoff is shown in the following graphic.

Adding Resource Capacity

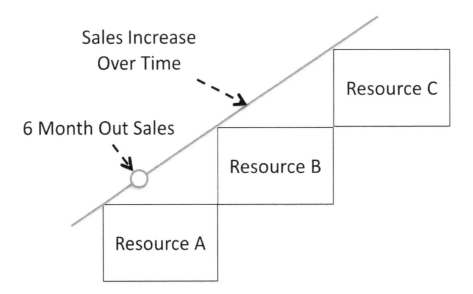

Resources ordinarily must be added as discrete units, while demand increases tend to be continuous. A pattern may be determined, and forecasted that eventually will require adding a resources in order to satisfy demand. However, when exactly these resources should be added can be up for debate. It can be possible to run the existing resource or resource overtime by adding labor and extending the factory operating hours. This can allow for the postponement of the purchase and installation of the resource until later when the demand has grown even more and the utilization of the resource is more or less guaranteed. Certainly the cost of the resource will play into this decision, as will the profitability of the product, which is produced on the resource.

Conclusion

Everyone seems to love talking about the opportunity of S&OP. However, the details of how to connect S&OP systems to the systems that supply them with information are not yet fully realized in current software. There are a number of important decisions to be made that influence how the S&OP process will be managed and what level of planning will be performed, as well as how much the existing planning results will be accepted versus being modified by the executives in the S&OP meeting. Secondly, modification on the part of executives will mean having to incorporate those changes back to the various lower-level plans.

This chapter was careful to point out that while S&OP literature, including this book admittedly tends to very strongly focus on S&OP for manufacturers and distributors. However, S&OP is just as much needed in service industries as the need to balance long-term supply and demand, and to perform long-term budgeting and capital improvement planning is universal. Two common questions for service companies are:

- How long should queues be allowed to grow?
- How long should processes like the opening of a new account be allowed to take?

The traditional approach to S&OP for manufacturers and distributors is to feed S&OP spreadsheets (which are normally developed internally by the company) the demand, supply and production plan, which is then dollarized. These plans are not simply the automated first planning output, but are the final plans that have been modified by demand, supply and production planners. Without very much in the way of discussion, some of the newer S&OP applications have broadened out their functionality to the point where they are able to create simplified plans that are already created in supply chain planning systems. However most companies still use spreadsheets for their S&OP process. The more complex and detailed the S&OP application, more categories of data that are sent to it from other systems and the more the S&OP application is able to do on its own. One of the major differentiators between the more traditional S&OP and the more modern S&OP is that the newer applications can capacity level specific resources within the S&OP application, rather than relying upon another system to do this and then send the output to the S&OP application.

The standard S&OP process is to review and sign off on the demand plan, review and sign off on the supply plan and review and sign off on the financial plan. The process begins by trying to develop a final forecast that is the combination of multiple forecasts, as there are multiple forecasts within any company.

When the S&OP system receives the supply plan, it may have been either constrained or capacity leveled. Resource management and constraining is one of the more complex areas of planning, however the objective is to develop a feasible plan. Over the short and perhaps medium-term the company must deal with the constraints that exist. That is the intent of supply chain planning. A big part of short and medium-term supply chain planning is simply moving production and procurement either forward or backwards along the planning timeline in order to eliminate situations of overcapacity. However, S&OP is planning over the long-term and, over the long-term, a company may choose to alter the constraints. While production resources are sometimes constrained or capacity-leveled by supply chain planning systems, the other supply planning focused resources (storage, location, shipping, transportation, etc.) tend not to be. This means that gaining a picture of the overload on these types of resources is much less straightforward. Most companies deal with these types of resources by feel (making educated guesses, based on the intuition of company planners).

This is one of the **myths** of S&OP processes, that all resources are modeled and become part of the S&OP process, allowing for evaluation. However, this is not the case. Even the most advanced supply chain planning applications tend not to focus on supply planning resources (aka, non-production) in isolation. Several software vendors show product demos featuring the management of these types of resources; however, given that this is uncommon even in applications with greater capabilities in the field of resource management, we doubt whether this is a realistic goal.

Finally, while the primary focus tends to be on resources, resources are only one of the constraints in planning, with another example being lot sizes or batch sizes. The final step of the S&OP process is reviewing and finalizing the financial plan. Financial plans are dependent upon the supply plan. For manufacturing and distribution companies, the first obvious financial implication is inventory. For a service company the obvious financial implication is the number of people required for a specific capacity. In addition to how much to increase capacity, a very important question that should come from the S&OP process is when to increase capacity. Almost all capacity is added in discrete rather than continuous units, however, demand tends to change in a continuous fashion, and secondly there is often a lag between the purchase of the capacity and when the capacity is available. The company wants to only add capacity that will have a high utilization, and this may mean doing everything from using outside sources of production, warehousing, etc. before deciding to actually purchase long-term capacity.

CHAPTER 3

S&OP Versus Integrated Business Planning

Integrated Business Planning, or IBP, from which the SAP product has taken its name, is a process which is a **superset** of S&OP. S&OP is technically simply one form of IBP. Wikipedia lists the following integrated planning processes as examples of IBP.

- Sales and Operations Planning

- Healthcare Analytics

- Strategic Corporate Performance Management

- Planning and scheduling across multiple plants in a factory

IBP integrates across two or more functions and the planning must result in **improving/optimizing financial value**.

Of the types of IBP listed above, *"planning and scheduling across multiple plants in a factory"* caught my eye. This must mean the planning and scheduling of multiple plants in a supply network, but the wording is unclear. Let's spend some time clearing the misconceptions in the use of the term IBP. Papers like *The Evolution from S&OP to Integrated Business Planning,* by Clarkston Consulting are one example of what I have found to be a **trend of entities proposing that IBP is a more advanced form of S&OP**. Here are several quotations from this paper.

> *"Many companies are now evolving from S&OP to Integrated Business Planning (IBP). IBP is a planning approach that incorporates the whole of the business enterprise with the goal to satisfy market demand while maximizing profitability.*
>
> *Compared to S&OP, IBP considers more factors, more functions and more opportunities, over a long-term, to help companies to better respondto internal and external factors.*
>
> *If you think about the traditional S&OP process, financials are considered, but are typically not a key driver for planning. Sitting on the operations side of the table, my team would receive the sales forecast and simply try to operationally execute on the projected customer demand. Strategically collaborating with Sales or Finance on critical financial considerations was just not a part of the standard process. In contrast, IBP brings additional people and criteria to the table.*
>
> *Additionally, the complexity and speed of today's marketplace forces companies to have a faster, more responsive and more integrated approach to planning. New product developments and launches, customers with unique demands, and evolving regulations are just a few of the continuously changing factors that highlight the shortcomings of traditional planning. These changes drivevariances that result in ad-hoc planning with Marketing, R&D, Regulatory and Finance.*

> *IBP is not a replacement for S&OP; instead, IBP incorporates and expands S&OP through increased scope, outlook and planning term. Independently, they both have the objective of satisfying demand, but IBP helps companies optimize business results through considering more factors, functions and opportunities over a long-term. These additional factors are incorporated into the S&OP process, which will continue to generate the tactical operations plan needed to run the business."*

This is the type of article that confuses readers as to the distinctions between IBP and S&OP, and this is a problem because an inadequate understanding of the definition of IBP leads people to declare that it's time to **move to IBP from S&OP**, giving the impression that IBP is some more advanced form of S&OP. This misunderstanding is nearly ubiquitous across the dozens of technical papers and articles I've read on the subject of IBP.

So let's go through the main points, because ideas similar to those proposed in this paper are sometimes proposed in other publications, so it is important to understand this line of thinking. Below I will explain why the statements in the quotations above are inaccurate.

- Plain old S&OP already incorporates the entire enterprise. Actually S&OP can be performed for any scope desired. To say that IBP is larger in scope than S&OP is untrue. IBP does not have a longer time horizon than S&OP. The S&OP planning horizon is as long as the company managing the S&OP process **desires it to be**. This is true whether the company uses a spreadsheet or anapplication for its S&OP process. Most of my clients have worked with an S&OP planning horizon of 24 months, butsome companies go out to 5 years. It should also be noted that companies choosing a short horizon for their S&OP process are likely doing so not because of limitations in S&OP, but because of limitations in their ability to accurately forecast demand. I would argue that a short horizon limits the utility of S&OP by preventing the company from making decisions that affect long-term planning, and that they should consider leaving their comfort zones, but this disagreement is not caused by a structural weakness in S&OP that is absent in IBP.

- IBP does not include more "factors" and more "opportunities." The point of S&OP is to include all factors and opportunities so that comprehensive decisions can be made.[1]

- If strategic collaboration with sales or finance on critical financial considerations was not part of the "standard process," for this particular company, then the company was not performing S&OP properly. Collaboration between sales, finance and operations, and on critical financial considerations is basically the definition of S&OP. IBP brings no further contributions to the table unless a company was not conducting a proper S&OP system. If finance or sales or operations were missing, then it was not S&OP.

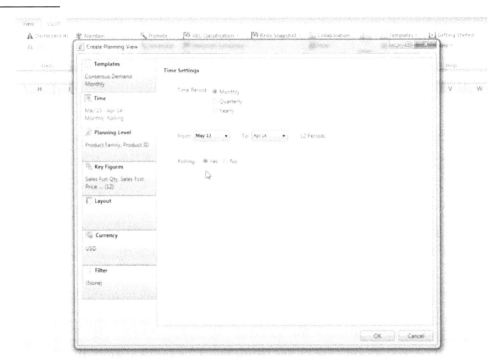

[1]

Notice, that as with any other planning system, the planning horizon can be set out as long as necessary. Now the set-planning horizon must match the horizon of the data, which is loaded. That is the forecasts that are loaded; the capacity value that is loaded must match the values that are in SAP IBP.

- S&OP is an integrated approach to planning. IBP is **not a "more" integrated** approach. In fact, S&OP is just one type of IBP. *"New product developments and launches and customers with unique demands"* does not promote IBP over S&OP. S&OP is already ready to handle all of these things. *"Evolving regulations"* also have nothing to do with promoting IBP over S&OP.

This white paper does not present a proper understanding of IBP or S&OP, and, therefore, only manages to add to the confusion of its readers. The overall theme of articles of this nature is to point out that S&OP is "limited" and that, therefore, a new process is required. Here is another quotation from a different article that confuses people, but from a different dimension.

> *"The breadth of planning covered in S&OP is also increasing. Many companies have moved from doing Sales & Operations Planning to Integrated Business Planning (IBP). In IBP, companies use the demand planning process to do not just unit forecasts, but also financial forecasts. While working to balance supply and demand, they seek to do that in a way that will also allow the company to meet the promises they have made to Wall Street.*
>
> *Once companies adopt Integrated Business Planning, which is the new best practice, other practices often follow. When the CFO becomes part of the IBP executive meeting, he may become interested in balancing supply and demand in a way that maximizes profits."*
> — Sales Operations Continues to Evolve

First of all, we've already seen, in this publication, that financial forecasting is the final product generated by any S&OP application or spreadsheet. To declare that financial forecasting is performed in IBP, in the way written, **implies that financial forecasting is not performed** in S&OP. Unit forecasts are performed in the supply chain planning process, but the S&OP forecasting process **always** dollarizes the forecast. If someone does not know that about S&OP, it is safe to assume they don't know much about S&OP.

Third, any CFO who regularly attended S&OP meetings, executed a "change" to an IBP process, and then, and only then, became interested in **balancing supply and demand in a way that maximizes profits** must not understand the subject of these meetings. That is the very definition of the S&OP process!

The general observations on the limitations of S&OP are entirely true, however, that has nothing to do with the **process of S&OP**. The process is sound; the problem is that getting executives from different groups to coordinate is very challenging, as is getting the necessary systems support. Secondly, not all groups are created equal, so the meetings between sales, finance and operations are not meetings of equals – and furthermore all these branches have difference incentives.

- Sales wants to maximize sales without much consideration for profitability.

- Finance wants to limit expenditures and wants as much as is feasible a guaranteed return on investment.

- Supply chain wants to limit the number of stock keeping units, reduce the number of manufacturing changeovers, and increase the forecast ability of the product database.

No process, or application, can alter these contradictory orientations. All of these goals are inconsistent with one another, so the question arises as to **who will get to impose their will upon the other groups**. For a long time, there were few good S&OP applications (something that has recently changed). Many companies have implemented an S&OP process without understanding what S&OP is. For example, one of my clients held an S&OP meeting that was simply a review of forecasts – and had nothing at all to do with capacity, supply planning or finance. Also, many companies engage in an S&OP process without actually having a quality supply chain or financial forecast or without having their capacity within a reasonable level of accuracy, which undermines the entire S&OP process. The problem of getting the top executives from the different major branches is **endemic and longstanding**, as is discussed in Chapter 7: Challenges in S&OP Implementation.

These difficulties should be acknowledged and then rectified, and simply coming up with another name for the same general process will not solve anything, although it may a good way to generate consulting revenue for some companies, it has little chance of accomplishing anything, **because it does not address the true inadequacies of the S&OP process as implemented at companies**. I fear that it is far easier to make money promoting a "new" thing than through putting in the work to improve an existing method in a meaningful way.

SAP's Naming of Their S&OP Application

Interestingly, while SAP named its S&OP product IBP, SAP IBP does not in fact perform the different areas of IBP outside of S&OP. For instance, IBP will not help in strategic corporate performance management. Therefore, it would seem that SAP IBP is actually misnamed and should have simply been called SAP S&OP. It's unclear to me why SAP named this application incorrectly, but if I had to guess, I would say it is because, currently, IBP is a "hotter" term in the marketplace.

Naming issues like this are not at all uncommon. For example, SAP has a planning product called EWM, which stands for extended warehouse management. However, an extended warehouse is an overflow warehouse, which is used when the main warehouse is over capacity. However, the EWM product is **not designed** for overflow warehouses, but is instead simply a more advanced warehouse management application versus the more basic SAP WM, which is part of the SAP ERP product. This misnaming does not normally have any impact on how the application is actually used. If one follows the correct use of the term, then one may ask why SAP IBP only performs the S&OP process. If one thinks of IBP incorrectly, as simply a "more involved" form of S&OP, then again, the individual will also be let down because SAP IBP only does S&OP. In short, the SAP IBP application is built to the S&OP business process.

CHAPTER 4

SAP IBP, ANAPLAN & SAP Cash Management

Any person who has experience with a planning system will feel comfortable with SAP IBP. In fact, SAP IBP is far easier to use than any other SAP planning application that I have seen before, and easier to configure as well. I would expect that any implementation consultant would spend less time configuring the system and more time managing the soft issues of enabling S&OP than any implementation of a planning module from SAP APO.

Interestingly, there is a rumor going around that SAP APO will be **replaced** by a combination of SAP IBP on HANA (sometimes shortened to the idea that HANA itself will replace SAP APO). I became aware of this rumor because I have been repeatedly asked this question by clients and by readers of my books and blog posts. So this seems to be a good place to address this. There are two main points to establish:

1. *HANA Replacing APO*: HANA cannot replace APO because HANA is infrastructure, and infrastructure cannot replace a business application. APO may be ported to HANA, but they are not competitive technologies.

2. *IBP Replacing APO*: APO has many modules that address all of the major supply chain planning areas within companies – from demand planning to warehouse management/planning. IBP is designed specifically for the S&OP planning process, which is a completely different process. This is not to say that IBP does not have some similar capabilities to APO, as I will cover, there is considerable overlap in several areas between IBP and APO. For instance, both IBP and APO can do statistical forecasting, and can show resource overloads, but IBP and APO have different purposes. Therefore IBP cannot replace APO as well as different depths of functionality in the areas where to do overlap..

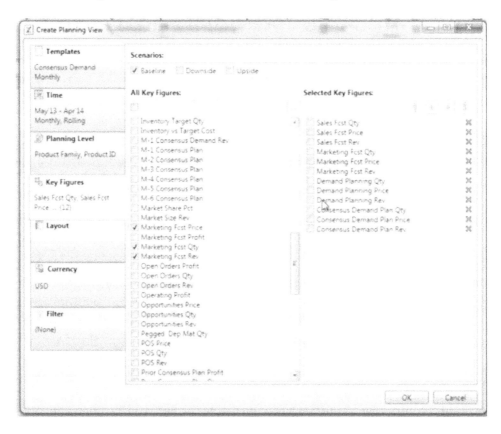

Key Figures is the term that SAP uses to describe the values that are shown in the user interface. Key Figures are also used in the SAP APO application, which performs supply chain planning. Here Key Figures can be added or removed by selecting the checkboxes. Different users will want to see different Key Figures, so the view can be customized by the user.

This shows that the currency can be changed, so that the same application can be used in different countries.

This shows a standard S&OP view which shows the predicted revenue per month.

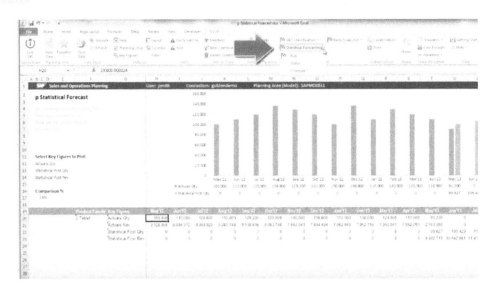

This screen shows that a statistical forecast is about to be created.

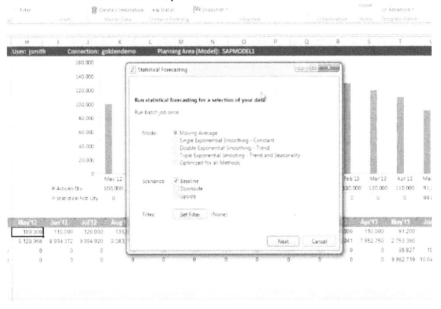

*Here the statistical forecasting options are shown. The options are: Moving Average, Single Exponential Smoothing, Constant, Single Exponential Smoothing, Trend, Triple Exponential Smoothing, Trend and Seasonality and a best fit, or optimized for all methods. This final option is a best fit, where the SAP IBP determines the best model to use. **Best-Fit forecasting** is covered in great detail in the SCM Focus Press book Forecast Parameters: Alpha, Beta Gamma, etc.*

SAP provides the ability to perform statistical forecasting within the application, or to load forecasts from an external forecasting system. **However, it brings up a pair of interesting questions**. There are a number of complex settings within SAP IBP that allow an assignment of a specific model with parameters to the options shown in the screen shot above. Who is qualified among executives to set those parameters and to assign them to the right aggregation, in order to generate a forecast? And if a forecast is generated within the S&OP system, and **is not the same** as the forecast generated by supply chain planning, then what is the correlation between the forecast generated in the IBP system and the supply chain forecast? Questions literally abound.

When a statistical forecast is generated in a supply chain planning system, it is normally manually adjusted. In general practice, because most companies have difficulty in mastering their statistical forecasting systems, there is quite a bit of manual intervention, even for products where a proper statistical forecast outperforms the manually adjusted forecast. However, if the statistical forecast is generated in IBP, none of these adjustments will be included (that are incorporated in the final forecast) and, therefore, the S&OP process will be working off of a forecast that may be significantly different from the forecast which is generated by the demand planning group. However, the forecast of the demand-planning group is the important forecast because those are the individuals that actually know every product. They know for when a product is being discontinued and when the standard statistical forecast cannot be used. This **also brings up the question of who should be performing the forecast** and is the forecasting work being duplicated or are executives overwriting work performed by demand planners. The answer to improving forecast accuracy is not having executives perform forecasting, which then has to be adjusted by demand planners. And this same issue applies to the supply and production side. For this topic, a story will provide the necessary context.

Once, on a factory visit, I was asked by one of the plant managers if I came from the *"Puzzle Palace."* I asked him what he meant by that, and he was referring to the headquarters, which was, indeed, my prior locale. *"He went on to tell me, I call it that because no one there knows what they are doing, and they are still trying to put together the pieces."* I have received this same "vibe" or similar indicators, from almost every manufacturing plant I've ever visited.

Most often, factory management do not think that the individuals in headquarters necessarily lack in intelligence, but that they are completely out of touch with what is happening in the factory. Here are two classic examples:

1. *Lot Sizing*: At one client, the materials management group spent a lot of time creating production lot sizes that were appealing for inventory management. These production lot sizes were then entered into the system and controlled the production plan. The factories received the production plan, found that they were completely uneconomic for production, creating multiple planning runs for the same product in a week. They then simply batched up the production orders themselves so that the facility produces the same quantity in a week, but in one production run.

2. *Supplier Constraint Modeling*: Companies often discuss how beneficial it would be if they could only model the constraints of their suppliers. However, this is a strange statement given that these same companies cannot even accurately model the constraints of their internal factories. To take advantage of all that the sophisticated software has to offer for managing resources, this situation will have to improve in the future. Therefore, if the factory does not think that the supply and production planners at the headquarters have a real picture of the factory capacity, then how close will executives be to the factory capacity as they only occasionally dabble in the topic during S&OP meetings?

In order for the S&OP process to be useful, it must work off of the same assumptions that drive the actual planning. So, if executives begin making changes that eventually affect the plan, there will often be issues in implementing that change. At several of my clients, the VP of Supply Chain dictated that all inventories would be reduced by a certain percentage and on other occasions that the safety stock in particular would come down across the board (that is for all products) by a certain percentage. This type of thing never ends well, because the VP of Supply Chain does not understand the implications for making these changes. A good example of this was a manufacturer that had quarterly drives to reduce inventory at the end of each quarter. This lead to a saw tooth pattern of production, where production would drop at the beginning of each quarter (as the production floor lacked adequate inventory) and then production would rise through the quarter, until the end, where the inventory was once again curtailed to meet inventory objectives. The company did not like this saw tooth pattern, and brought me in to look at whether their production planning and scheduling application was malfunctioning.

S&OP is a more abstract version of the planning that is being performed continually at a more disaggregated level; problems with an S&OP system are almost always related to problems further upstream.

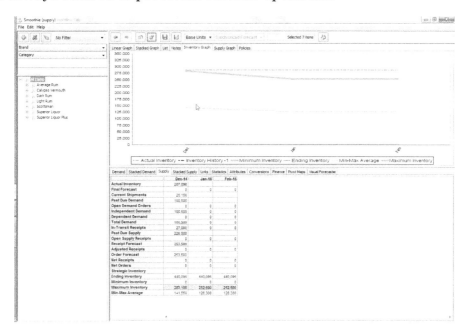

Here, the supply planner has developed scenarios that can help the company meet an unexpected demand. The options are: Increase Capacity in House (which would be new capital request), Short New Demand (which will require no investment, but could have a negative effect on future demand from this customer, as well as the loss of the revenue from the customer for the orders that are to be postponed or deleted), Use a Contract Manufacturer (requires no new capital, but will result in a lower margin in most cases, as the contract manufacturer is a backup to the internal manufacturing).

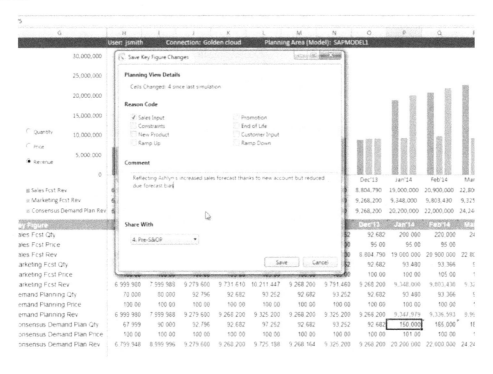

Here, a forecast is driven to see the effect on supply. Then a note is added to explain what assumptions are included in this scenario.

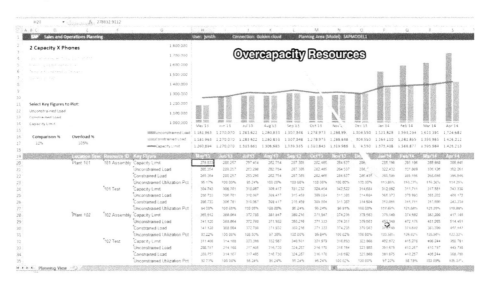

This shows that resources within factories can be identified as overcapacity. Although obvious, I would like to add that this means that resources data must be added to the

IBP system. I generally don't see this level of detail within S&OP processes. However, I have seen something very similar through the use of a custom spreadsheet that allowed resources to be quickly updated. This means tying the demand to each product, which is then assigned to each resource. This is already in the supply and or production planning system that a company would have. However, to do what is shown above, it means having these relationships in SAP IBP as well. It means integrating this data between the supply chain planning system and SAP IBP.

Resource Adjustments Performed in the S&OP Application?

Resource planning is presented as very straightforward in SAP IBP. However, resource management in SAP APO is actually quite complex and different resources can be setup as time-continuous, or bucket, or mixed resources (mixed resources can be used by both supply planning and production planning). There are also single-activity resources versus multi-activity resources. There are different resource types (storage, transportation, manufacturing, etc.), and they have complex master data that needs to be set just so in order to work properly. Some of this workload can be reduced if there is integration between SAP IBP and SAP APO; however, there are always adjustments that are necessary in any application that is performing the planning processing. The only group that would have the background to adjust and troubleshoot these resources within the company would be the group that is supporting SAP APO or any other advanced planning application. Therefore SAP IBP is now maintenance overhead for this group. An important question would be whether this group will receive extra funding in order to support this extra application if it is purchased.

Resource level adjustments tend to occur within the planning system. If they are also made in SAP IBP, and if they are performed by resource, then there begins to become an overlap and a **duplication of some of the work**. This is important to avoid doing because there is always a shortage of planning capacity within companies, too few demand planners, too few supply planners, etc. Furthermore, companies also tend to run very lean on the type of support that understands the planning system at a detailed level that can help tune the system and improve its usage and allow users to tune the necessary functionality. Therefore, I think there are questions to be raised about how detailed the S&OP process should be. After all, the more detailed those plans get, the more overhead and the more consumption of resources from the traditional planning processes will ensue.[1]

It is very easy to view the screen shown above and to underestimate the complexity involved in resource planning, and the complexity very much depends upon the complexity of the manufacturing floor. Consultants often like to talk about a straightforward production line for discrete manufacturing (discrete being cars, pens, bicycles, etc.), but lots of manufacturing companies do not have such a straightforward setup. Process industry manufacturing, for example, has much more complex interactions between the resources. A good example of this is that process industries often have variable output based upon a fixed input, or the operations may lag one another. Another issue is the question of resource interchangeability. For example, a simpler design is when there is **no resource** interchangeability on the manufacturing floor. The following graphic illustrates this scenario.

---

[1] Resource accuracy should always be considered, and never accepted as being accurate simply because number have been assigned to resource capacity. This is because many companies do not maintain adequate databases on the history of work center and resource capacities or their sequence. This information is needed to set up the model correctly. Secondly, few companies are willing to make the effort to constantly update these resource constraints as things change in the supply chain.

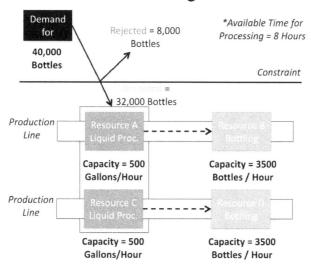

In this case, there is a single pathway for the manufacturing process.

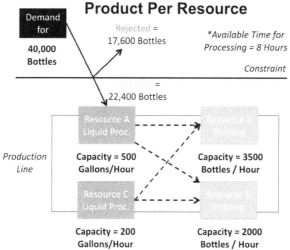

However, in this case, the bottling resources of B and D can both service the liquid processing resources of A and C. The more complex the resource interactions, the more difficult it is to present or model in the S&OP modeling tool.

Production Alternatives

Another complexity which is not only an issue SAP IBP, but for supply and production planning systems is that companies often have a number of external options or possess external capacity that they can call upon. This can be subcontractors or contract manufactures. Modeling the capacity of an external entity is a problem area for planning systems, as planning systems are not designed to represent external entities as if they are internal entities.

I have reviewed the SAP IBP demo and it looks too easy, which most likely slips by most executive decision makers. I can easily imagine a software vendor using a simple discrete manufacturing resource model to show a potential client how "easy it is to model manufacturing" in their S&OP application, and the client getting a big surprise when the try to model *their* resources during the implementation.

Now that we have covered SAP IBP a bit, let's move onto another S&OP vendor.

Here we have a few examples from Anaplan's S&OP application (which they call an app). It is one of the most attractive applications in the S&OP space.

Country Plan			Global Plan		
1.	Country Plan Summary	- View product level country plan vs. global target	6.	Global Target Summary	- View yearly sales and profit targets - Compare growth % by country
2.	Price Input	- Configure sales price increase at category and brand level - View YoY sales price growth	7.	Sales Target Set	Define yearly global sales targets
3.	Volume Input	- Set volume growth on market assumptions - Run market growth and share scenarios	8.	Net Sales Summary	- Analyze yearly sales growth by geo - Compare product yearly sales targets
4.	Brand Positioning Summary	Examine product's position within the market	9.	Target Allocation by Brand & Innovation	- Define target allocation by brand - Measure incremental sales from new product innovation
5.	Advertising & Promotion Input	- Create A&P cost assumptions based on market position	10.	Target Allocation by Country	- View target allocation by geo based on historical YoY growth
			11.	Profit Margin Target Set	- Define yearly P&O margin targets

Here we can see how Anaplan allows the individual to go right into the area that is applicable. After changes have been made at the regional level, they roll up to the levels above this automatically.

Country Plan			Global Plan		
1.	Country Plan Summary	- View product level country plan vs. global target	6.	Global Target Summary	- View yearly sales and profit targets - Compare growth % by country
2.	Price Input	- Configure sales price increase at category and brand level - View YoY sales price growth	7.	Sales Target Set	Define yearly global sales targets
3.	Volume Input	- Set volume growth on market assumptions - Run market growth and share scenarios	8.	Net Sales Summary	- Analyze yearly sales growth by geo - Compare product yearly sales targets
4.	Brand Positioning Summary	Examine product's position within the market	9.	Target Allocation by Brand & Innovation	- Define target allocation by brand - Measure incremental sales from new product innovation
5.	Advertising & Promotion Input	- Create A&P cost assumptions based on market position	10.	Target Allocation by Country	- View target allocation by geo based on historical YoY growth
			11.	Profit Margin Target Set	- Define yearly P&O margin targets

Here we can see that the market growth can be adjusted, which of course adjusts the forecast. However, while that is interesting, the executives should not be changing the assumptions regarding market growth, at least in anything but a simulation. That is to be determined by those with the **domain expertise**. *Those individuals – most likely from Sales, will have spent a great deal of time adjusting the forecast, or debating with Operations how to apply this input, and one of the background assumptions is the market growth estimate.*

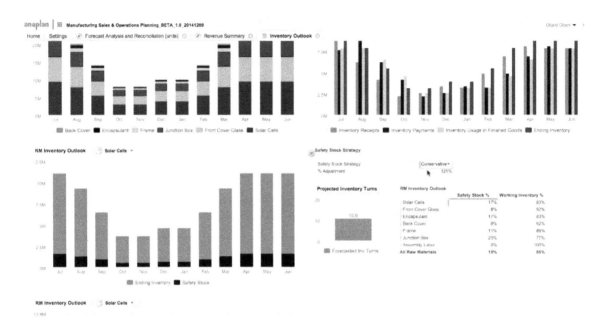

Here we have a strange setting. The safety stock can be adjusted to "Conservative" or "Aggressive," which changes the safety stock assumption to different percentages of the current safety stock. However, nowhere does it show a connection to service level, and safety stock cannot be adjusted as though it were a global variable, because the characteristics of the various products are different. Safety stock needs to be correlated to service levels, and the only sub-category of software that has the ability to do this is called inventory optimization and multi-echelon planning.

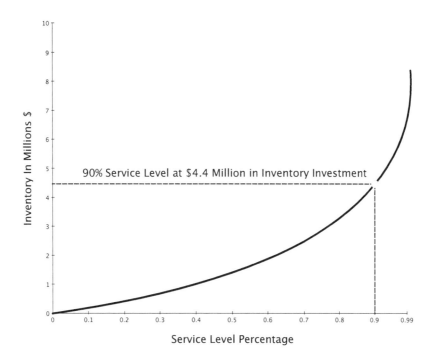

This graphic has been seen at one time or another by most supply chain professionals, and it demonstrates the fact that companies must decide what levels of service they can afford and, most importantly, what levels of service their customers are willing to pay for.

Inventory optimization and multi-echelon planning software (MEIO for short) is able to accurately calculate the relationship between service level and inventory because it has the specialized mathematics to perform this activity. The relationship between inventory and service levels is non-linear; higher and higher service levels require disproportionate increases in inventory to support them. The closer service levels come to one hundred percent, the more extreme the costs become. How service levels are set within companies is its own detailed topic, but, to make a long story short, most companies do not know the quantitative relationship between service level and inventory, and there is considerable "fudging" of the service levels metrics into order to bring the company's service level "in line" with its goals. The SCM Focus Press book *Inventory Optimization and Multi Echelon Software*, covers all of these topics in great detail.

Having functionality within S&OP applications to simply change safety stock across the board, and which has no connection to output or to service levels, may look advanced and sexy but it's not beneficial for executives to simply change safety stock levels in aggregate just so they can "see" what happens (well I supposed they can see what happens, but they should be careful about accepting this). This could be a recipe for the executives determining that safety stock should be brought down because the S&OP system will allow them to save so much inventory money from doing this.

Cash Forecasting

S&OP is an input to the financial forecasting and budgeting process. Effectively managing financial resources means knowing the needs of your company in the short, medium and long-term. Does the company have extra cash in the short-term? How long until the cash is projected to be needed, as excess cash can be invested? As this is a book on S&OP, the focus is more on the long-term, although certainly medium-term investment and budgeting decisions could also be made with S&OP software. S&OP is a process that still has **quite a lot of overhead**, requiring frequent meetings. These meetings are necessary because software in this area is not currently sufficiently sophisticated to allow for the process to be managed by people simply logging into a system and performing analysis.

Let's engage in a thought experiment for a moment. In an integrated system with the right functionality, finance could simply see the financial implications of the plans by logging into the company's system. Let's imagine that a company was increasing its sales by 30% over the next year, and this required new resources to be brought into new factories or even new factories to be built. Under an optimal scenario, this would **all be modeled in the company's system**. Finance could simply review the planning horizon, focusing on periods of time where the business may be requesting too much money, and then bringing particular investment questions up through messaging within the application. For instance, new factories would show as coming up say 6 months hence. Finance could then approve or disapprove of the new factory through the system. This is a concept, of course; systems aren't anywhere close to being able to do this. However, what does exist is short-term financial forecasting based upon financial documents. Within both the financial module of ERP systems and specialized financial applications like FinancialForce, finance and accounting can see a very complete picture of their predicted inflows and outflows. In SAP, this functionality is called Cash Management, and it resides in the SAP ERP system in the Treasury sub-module of Financial Accounting and Controlling. Cash Management is **not part** of the S&OP process, but it is conceptually interesting in that determining short-term financial flows is far more automated, and this is why I wanted to include this topic in the book.

Short-term financial planning is more cut and dried than long-term. For short-term budgeting, invoices of certain dollar amounts and certain dates of payment are submitted by the company to its customers, and its suppliers submit other known invoices to the company. Questions of investing in extra capacity, whether a demand forecast is likely to be correct or not, are not at issue.

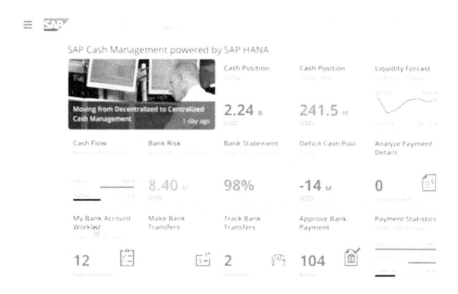

This user screen provides a view into the important high-level key performance indicators that a financial and accounting individual would be interested in knowing.

This shows the actual cash position per country, and provides warnings where cash may be running short. Using this information, the financial resource planner may decide to make adjustments. This application has the adjustments that must be made, such as withdrawing funds from a bank built into the application and performing a wire transfer.

Due to the simpler decision-making framework, and the fact that shorter-term financial activities are represented in the system through active transactions, like invoices and account postings, it is much easier for accountants to perform the activities of cash management in more or less isolation from the rest of the company. S&OP, which has a strong budgeting focus, cannot be performed in isolation because there are too many interactions, issues that require clarification, probabilities to be weighed, etc.

Conclusion

This chapter was designed to provide explanation as to how some S&OP applications work, and explain the relationship between financial forecasting and budgeting in the short-term (and the systems that might be used) versus long-term financial forecasting and budgeting that requires input from the S&OP process. In the case of SAP IBP, because SAP IBP is such a detailed application, there is overlap between the functionality contained in IBP and the functionality contained within supply chain planning applications. Therefore it would be very easy to use SAP IBP to essentially undermine the planning activity, which is performed by individuals with much more understanding of the details than is available to the executives. This brings up an interesting conversation as to **who** uses SAP IBP and what they use it for, which is of course critical to getting value from the system. Something which I am not seeing sufficiently addressed in material on SAP IBP, or in articles on S&OP in general is that to have a successful S&OP process, it's important to build in so much detail into the application that requires so much overhead that the company cannot reasonably be expected to maintain the application.

Companies that use Anaplan's S&OP application face the same issue. For instance, Anaplan provides the ability to adjust the forecast, however, it is an open question whether the people that are involved in the S&OP process have the domain expertise to override forecasts that have been made lower in the organization by planners who have a far better feel for what the forecast should be? In the articles, and certainly in the marketing material of S&OP vendors, these issues aren't brought up, and much of the literature on S&OP treats applications as if they are roughly the same in their scope, when in fact, as has been shown already, the scope is quite different depending upon the particular application or spreadsheet used. How any particular company chooses to answer the question I posed above – what should and should not be modeled by S&OP – determines what sort of software they should purchase.

CHAPTER 5

The Impact of SAP IBP With HANA

HANA is infrastructure upon which SAP applications run. HANA has been the subject of probably the most aggressive push by a software vendor in the history of enterprise software. For years, marketing messages on SAP were so all-encompassing that, when you got a number of SAP consultants in a room, each one had a different opinion of what HANA actually was. HANA is a data infrastructure which is optimized for analytics and is a database design that is optimized for memory over spinning disks, and it is part of an overall trend where analytics have become enormously popular in all manner of information technology conferences.

Books have been written on HANA, but there is still a lot of confusion as to how to effectively use it. There is also confusion why SAP makes such an emphasis on HANA when the issues that HANA addresses are not the primary issues that companies face with their SAP applications. Some people say that it should primarily be used for analytical or business intelligence applications, while others say that the whole point is to place applications like ERP on HANA so that specialized reporting applications that sit on their own hardware become unnecessary. I routinely hear opinions on HANA and how it will impact SAP planning that I find problematic. In this chapter we will get into this topic which should be helpful to those that work at companies that run SAP.

What is SAP HANA?

HANA is a memory resident database that leverages solid state drives and RAM, so applications run faster, but of course this hardware is more expensive as are the resources required to assemble it. HANA is also a columnar database, which means that instead of using a relational design – a series of tables that point to one another through primary keys – in HANA, every table is a single column and of course this leads to many more tables with many more interconnections. There are specific advantages to this design particularly for analytical applications, and in particular when the database design is used in conjunction with a RAM and solid state device memory.

A number of years after HANA has been introduced, it is still not all that common in SAP clients. The pitch is that, with HANA, applications like IBP will be able to able to perform so fast that all types of better analysis are now possible. Back in the 1990's, the software vendor i2 Technologies (for whom I used to be employed) promised that memory resident planning systems combined with mathematical optimizers would be game changers in supply and production planning. This turned out not to be case. Later SAP introduced APO with its liveCache, another memory resident database and it was going to superpower APO to new great speed improvements. Alas, the speed improvements weren't really any greater than what I found in other applications that used a more traditional hardware design. Every new introduction is inflated in magnitude by its natural marketing push. Thus, the only way to be sure about bold claims is to perform testing.

Taking a Holistic View of Applications

The proposal is that S&OP requires super-fast response and processing times, and therefore SAP IBP really needs to run on HANA. But processing speed is not the only potential drain on overhead and time for a company in search of an S&OP solution. The complex design of SAP IBP, which replicates the planning work usually done in a supply chain/demand modeling application, will, for many companies, result in increased overhead even if it processes the data more rapidly. If you have specialists doing things like capacity leveling, making projections for demand, and creating supply plans, and then you turn that information over to executives without the same domain expertise, and their application allows them to overwrite that work, you could wind up wasting a lot of money while, at the same time, producing suboptimal S&OP plans. In reality, my clients have had some of their best successes on radically simpler tools like DemandWorks Smoothie because the system has a much less imposing learning curve and is easier to maintain, with far less overhead.

Therefore, while this is not a chapter designed to merely be critical of placing S&OP on a faster hardware platform, but rather to point out that the impacts of using different software cannot be simply assumed to be superior because of a faster hardware platform or because of other "leading edge" factors that may be mentioned by software vendors. Instead the ability of the application to demonstrate the ability to work in the way that the company wants to work with its S&OP process is a far better predictor of the benefits the company will gain from the software.

CHAPTER 6

S&OP, Aggregation, and Forecast Hierarchies

S&OP is an aggregated planning process. Therefore, one of the major questions, when engaging in S&OP planning, is the right level of the hierarchy in which to plan the process. This is explained in the following quotation.

> *"One of the hottest discussion points during the (re)design of an S&OP process is the level of detail. While some people strive to the highest possible detail, others push to look only at global figures. Both parties have a point. The "detailists" often argue that it is impossible to check the impact of certain constraints, such as production constraints or customer requirements on a global level. As a result, they aim for a plan on customer-article level. The "globalists" position themselves on the other side of the spectrum, arguing that S&OP should only look at the big lines. They conclude that S&OP should operate on 4 or 5 big product families."*
>
> – Sales and Operations Planning, How to
> Avoid the 5 Key Pitfalls

71

This article proposes that S&OP is between Strategic Planning (Define Capital Investment to Achieve Long-term Goals) and Master Planning (Aligning Operational Resources to Meet Orders and Forecasts), and that it is important that S&OP be linked to both of these other processes. This bring up the topic of assigning responsibilities and understanding the scope of the S&OP process and decisions that are made in the S&OP process.

> *"An example will make this clearer: at a company in the food ingredients business, the management wondered why the S&OP process had so little impact on operations. In our analysis, we found that the S&OP team spent a lot of effort defining which part of the European market would be delivered to from each of the European plants. In reality, however, customer orders were allocated to plants based on the same basic rules every month. The company had no way to impose the S&OP sourcing on the order entry process. Only when the company implemented an automated interface between the S&OP results and the company's transactional system did the S&OP process get a real grip on operations. From that moment onwards, it gained respect from the different departments involved and it became a real management tool."*
>
> – Sales and Operations Planning, How to
> Avoid the 5 Key Pitfalls

Attribute-based Forecasting and Virtual Hierarchies

Attribute-based forecasting is the use of a product's attributes to create "virtual hierarchies." An attribute can be anything that is associated with a product. It can be a physical product attribute such as the color or size of an item. However, it can also be any categorization of a product that the company chooses to model in the forecasting software. In the right software, adding attributes is so easy. I have experimented with performing attribute forecasting in a way I have never seen documented. In lifecycle planning, attributes can be used to categorize products by their phase of life, and to apply an adjustment to a product grouping. Another major use of attribute-based forecasting is to perform top-down forecasting, or forecasting based upon aggregations. Top-down forecasting forecasts for a grouping of products and eventually disaggregates down to the SKU based upon some disaggregation logic (which can be adjusted in some applications). Forecasts based upon aggregations tend to be more accurate, demonstrate seasonality and trends more clearly, and possess less bias. Different groups of products or channels will be optimally forecasted at different aggregation levels and/or using different hierarchies. More on this topic is provided in the link below:

http://www.scmfocus.com/demandplanning/2010/07/pivot-forecasting-rendersforecast- hierarchies-obsolete/

Attribute-based forecasting makes it possible to forecast each segment of a business with the attribute that works best for improving forecast accuracy. Static hierarchy systems can also produce top-down forecasts. However, they can only produce them along the static levels that exist in the hierarchy. In order to select the right attributes on which to perform top-down forecasting, various attributes must be tested. Static hierarchy systems are not designed to test attributes. (Attribute testing can also be performed in an external mathematical environment such as Oracle Crystal Ball, but this is done infrequently.) Therefore, the most common situation is for a company to have a static hierarchy setup, which does not include a level that improves the forecast accuracy when performing a top-down forecast. Many companies that I have worked with are simply not aware that attributes can be tested to determine which ones improve the forecast.

Attributes in Demand Works Smoothie

I have used Demand Works Smoothie in order to explain how attribute forecasting works. More information on how Demand Works performs attribute-based forecasting is provided at the link below:

http://www.scmfocus.com/demandplanning/2011/05/flexible-attribute-selection- in-smoothie/

Smoothie can be fed data from a database when the application is being used as a live production system, or it can read data from a preformatted spreadsheet when being used on a stand-alone system. The spreadsheet is eventually imported into an SQL database used by the Smoothie application. I demonstrate Smoothie in this stand-alone mode as I am dealing with a small amount of data. This spreadsheet is easy for me to adjust and to show screen shots of the data setup along with how the attributes are shown in the user interface. Regardless of the mode in which Smoothie is used, one attribute is represented as a column. You will see multiple columns representing multiple attributes in the Smoothie spreadsheet.

Adjusting Smoothie's Virtual Hierarchy

While attribute-based forecasting does not have a static hierarchy in the database, it emulates a hierarchy in the user interface. The hierarchy is simply presented to the user as a visual element, the same way it would be presented in a static hierarchy system, except that the user has the ability to adjust the hierarchy based upon any of the attributes that have been added to the database. In Smoothie, hierarchies are only temporary because they are simply a flexible sequence of relational objects. (For this reason the term *attribute sequence* is more accurate than the term *hierarchy*. But because it is completely unknown, the term must be explained the first few times it is used.) Attribute sequences can be shown graphically, but there is really no better way to demonstrate the concept than going directly to the application.

Attributes have to be selected in the interface in order to display properly. Choose the attributes by selecting the drop down selection boxes, and then refresh by choosing the "thunderbolt" icon. This is the attribute sequence or virtual hierarchy that I have been discussing up to this point. To change the hierarchy, simply select different attributes in a different sequence, and select the thunderbolt icon again. The following screenshots demonstrate how quickly a virtual hierarchy can be changed without requiring any changes to the underlying data.

Notice the attribute sequence is Location – Ice Cream Type – Flavor – Size. This is defined in the upper left hand corner of the interface where attributes and their sequence are defined. However, the attribute sequence, as well as what attributes appear in the virtual hierarchy, is infinitely changeable.

Now, we will adjust the hierarchy by simply selecting the attribute drop down as is shown on the following page.

We have now "created" an entirely new hierarchy. Notice that now the attribute sequence is Location – Ice Cream Type – Size – Flavor. The Size and Flavor attributes were switched, but any attribute combination is possible.

Smoothie can have an enormous number of attributes (over two hundred), but most companies typically use between five and fifteen attributes, including product, channel or customer, organization, region and classification data. Each group of users will typically focus on a particular subset of attributes and in differing orders according to their roles. All participants and departments can use the same application and the same data files to see their own virtual hierarchies by selecting and sequencing them in the user interface. All of this can be accomplished simply and without anyone stepping on anyone else's toes. Different forecast results can also be accomplished by having different groups store their results in different measures.

This screen shot shows a universal need across analytical systems, not only for forecasting. This is described by the analytical graphics book, Now You See It: Simple Visualization Techniques for Quantitative Analysis.

It's frequently useful to navigate through information from a high level to progressively lower levels in a defined hierarchical structure and back up again. This is what I described earlier as "drilling." A typical example involves sales analysis by region along a defined geographical hierarchy, such as continents at the highest level, then countries, followed by states or provinces, and perhaps down to cities at the lowest level. On the following page, the node-link diagram (also known as a tree diagram) illustrates a familiar way to display hierarchies.

Creating the Attributes in the Application Database

It is very simple to create attributes in Smoothie. Any attribute must be represented as a column in the Smoothie input file. The number of combinations of attributes (planning items) that can be added is limited primarily by hardware sizing. Attributes are simply added as columns in the Attribute tab of the spreadsheet (when being used in demo mode), or within a table (when used in a production environment).

	A	B	C	D	E	F	G	H
1	SKU	WHSE	Description	Location Description	DC Type	Ice Cream Type	Flavor	Size
2	NVHP	1	Ice Cream	San Diego	DC 1	Normal	Vanilla	Half Pint
3	NVP	1	Ice Cream	San Diego	DC 1	Normal	Vanilla	Pint
4	ERVHP	1	Ice Cream	San Diego	DC 1	Extra Rich	Vanilla	Half Pint
5	ERVP	1	Ice Cream	San Diego	DC 1	Extra Rich	Vanilla	Pint
6	NCHP	1	Ice Cream	San Diego	DC 1	Normal	Chocholate	Half Pint
7	NCP	1	Ice Cream	San Diego	DC 1	Normal	Chocholate	Pint
8	ERCHP	1	Ice Cream	San Diego	DC 1	Extra Rich	Chocholate	Half Pint
9	ERCP	1	Ice Cream	San Diego	DC 1	Extra Rich	Chocholate	Pint
10	NCDHP	1	Ice Cream	San Diego	DC 1	Normal	Cookie Dough	Half Pint
11	NCDP	1	Ice Cream	San Diego	DC 1	Normal	Cookie Dough	Pint
12	ERCDHP	1	Ice Cream	San Diego	DC 1	Extra Rich	Cookie Dough	Half Pint
13	ERCDP	1	Ice Cream	San Diego	DC 1	Extra Rich	Cookie Dough	Pint

Being able to store, manipulate and upload product and attributes files from a single spreadsheet with multiple tabs is in my view a best practice and is described in the post below:

http://www.scmfocus.com/demandplanning/2011/05/a-better-way-ofimporting-data-into-forecasting-and-analytic-systems/

To find out more detail on this topic see the link below, which shows Smoothie's capabilities in this area, and how it enables flexible management of attributes.

http://www.scmfocus.com/demandplanning/2011/05/flexible-attribute-selection-in-smoothie/

Forecasting by Customer

As stated, an attribute can be any categorization that one wants to associate with a product. An attribute can also be a customer. There are several ways of associating a customer with a product. Coding the product per customer would not make a lot of sense, as only one customer per product would be allowed and nothing would be aggregated. The following three coding methods would work much better:

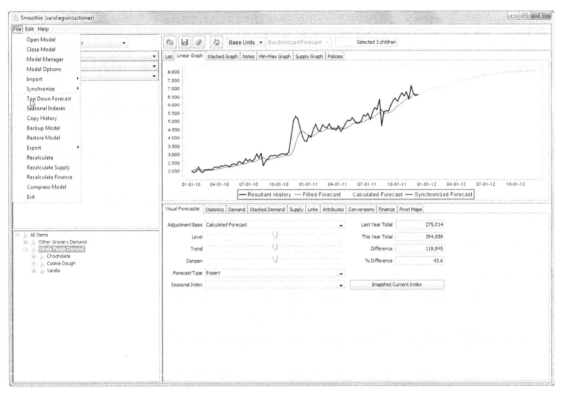

Above we have assigned two attributes, one for Other Grocery Demand and one for Whole Foods Demand. As this company sells fifty percent of its product to Whole Foods, it makes sense to develop a forecast and an attribute for just this customer. Using multiple customer attributes would allow for aggregated forecasting by customer. Not every customer would necessarily be entered into the attribute columns—possibly only critical or large customers. The maximum number of attribute columns required would be the maximum number of customers that would be applied to any product. The second method, customer groups, would require less attribute setup but would also provide less flexibility. It would only allow aggregation based upon a grouping of customers and not just one customer. The third method would focus on breaking out only large customers.

Performing the Top-down Forecast

In addition to viewing the forecast by the attribute, top-down forecasting can be performed by any attribute. This is accomplished in Smoothie from the menu I have selected **File –> Top-Down Forecast** in the screen shot below. Next, select the attribute and then the measure where you want to place the forecast.

This is a very simple way to perform a top-down forecast. Creating a top-down forecast on the basis of attributes is highly recommended because the attributes are so flexible, and attributes other than those that are "officially recognized" can be used. "Customer" was used as an example, but any attribute can be used as is demonstrated in Chapter 11: "Lifecycle Planning." Being able to alter and add attributes in this flexible manner is a tool that demand planners can adjust and improve their usage of over time.

There are options for different levels of detail when creating a forecast in this way. For instance, an attribute coding system can be created for the largest customers, while the other customers are nondifferentiated. Differentiating between customers can be very beneficial if larger customers have significant differences in their behavior and forecast accuracy than smaller customers.

Having the ability to forecast by attributes allows these types of modeling questions to be asked. And, this modeling flexibility applies to all attributes.

Forecasting by the Customer and Service Level Agreements

One benefit of attribute-based forecasting is that it allows a forecast and forecast aggregations to be created by customer or customer group. This forecast can later be recombined into a single line item per product location for use in standard supply planning applications. Doing so synchronizes the forecast aggregation type with how the supply plan is managed.

The ability to forecast by customer supports a growing trend in industry of managing the supply plan by customer. Many companies are contractually obligated to manage the supply plan by customer through something called "service level agreements," or SLAs, which define a specific service level to a customer for a specific level of compensation. SLAs are branching out from where they first developed in service organizations and are becoming popular in finished goods companies. I cover SLAs and their impact on supply planning in the book, *Inventory Optimization and Multi-Echelon Planning Software*. Inventory optimization and multi-echelon planning software is the only category of supply planning software designed to control the supply plan on the basis of the customer. Forecasting by customer can be an important complement to inventory optimization and multiechelon planning on the supply side.

Can Multi-attribute Forecasting Be Performed?

Different attributes or aggregations can be beneficial for different products. Smoothie allows different products to be forecasted by different attributes. Topdown forecasting can be performed for an attribute subgroup by using the Visual Forecasting tab, selecting the Calculated Forecast measure (even if it is already selected) as the adjustment basis, and then selecting the Save button. The topdown forecast is created for the selection. Next the forecast can be locked so that subsequent top-down forecasts using other attributes will not change these original forecast values. The product database can be sectioned off by previously-forecasted items and new forecast attributes used. That is the easy part. The complex part is performing the attribute testing to know which attributes work for which product groupings. This means segmenting the product database and testing attributes for the different segments.

Forecast Disaggregation

Every statistical forecasting vendor that I am aware of states that they can perform forecast aggregation and disaggregation; however, there is a large gap between statistical forecasting vendors in terms of capability. This functionality is too important for clients to simply accept the statement from a vendor that "our product can do that." In fact, aggregation and disaggregation should both be extensively demonstrated and tested by the company's planners prior to selecting an application for purchase, in order to discern how easy the aggregation functionality is to use in competing systems. Aggregation and disaggregation capability cannot be an afterthought. Instead these capabilities must be designed into the application from the database layer up. The following quote on this topic is instructive:

> *The allocations are according to each item's forecast which can be modified (to give them a larger or smaller share of the top-level changes) or locked (so that changes are only allocated to non-locked items). It's the way it's supposed to do it. The trick with Smoothie is the flexibility, ease and speed that we can handle these types of changes.*
>
> — Bill Tonetti, Demand Works

A comparison of forecast aggregation and disaggregation in two forecasting systems can be found at the link below:

http://www.scmfocus.com/demandplanning/2011/03/forecast-disaggregation-in-smoothie-vs-sap-dp/

Being able to aggregate effectively has many implications, some of which are not obvious. The following quote relates to how top-down forecasting supports improvements in the forecasting of seasonal products:

> *Statistical forecasts generated at a low level tend to have a positive bias. They can also miss seasonality and trends that are apparent at the aggregate levels. Patterns that are obvious at aggregate levels are masked by the stochastic behavior of demand at lower levels. The Top-down function prepares automated forecasts by aggregating*

demand streams according to any attribute in the model. As a result,
they are much more useful as a comparative statistical baseline than
only calculating and comparing the forecast at the base.

— Smoothie Help

Increasing or Decreasing the Forecast for a Product Group by Attribute

I have described how to perform a top-down forecast on the basis of an attribute. However, attributes can also be used to categorize products and then to apply changes, increases or decreases to things like trend or level, to the entire attribute grouping. Because attributes can be flexibly created and assigned, the grouping can be literally anything. For instance, let's say a company provides a variety of products that also includes storm gear. The forecast is for better weather. The company can isolate the storm gear products from the other products, and categorize and decrease them by a percentage, which is the expected decline of their sales. The regression formula can be created outside of the application in Excel, and the change in weather can be shown to decrease sales by a certain percentage based on the regression formula. This percentage increase or decrease can be applied to the attribute grouping. Applying some causal forecasting to products is far less maintenance than switching products to complete causal forecasting.

The Pros and Cons of Detailed Planning

Eventually, detailed planning must be performed. However, there is a tradeoff. Executives are most comfortable with an aggregated level of planning, and S&OP is an **executive planning process**. However, one cannot determine what is actually feasible if the process is kept aggregated. That is to say, one cannot drive to feasibility if one stays only at an aggregated level. For example, if one performs planning at the product family level, and the components of the product family are made using multiple different resources, without knowledge of demand for each member of the product family, there is insufficient detail to conduct adequate supply planning.

System Overlap and Planning Domain Expertise

There are really two major issues that bear on the question of aggregation level in a good S&OP model. The first is the overlap between supply and demand planning and the S&OP application. The second is the question of who is handling S&OP and whether they have domain expertise to do detailed planning on their own. Let's look at each issue.

1. *The Question of Planning Overlap*: S&OP software should not attempt to give the impression that it is replicating the planning that occurs in the supply chain planning applications. For instance, production-planning systems have incorporated setup data into the planning run. The setup information is designed to allow for feasible and optimal production sequences – say, moving the production sequence from lighter paints to darker paints before scheduling a cleanup which will result in the lowest possible downtime. Without this setup data, a system will assume there is no downtime between manufacturing changeovers, which a) is untrue, and b) will result not only in an incorrect or unrealistic production sequence, but **also in dangerous overestimates of true capacity**. If the S&OP system accepts the supply and production plan from the supply chain planning system, then it leverages this detail. Most seasoned analysts would tell you that sacrificing some ability to adjust the S&OP model in exchange for more realistic projections produced by trained professionals with access to details not generally possessed by executives is the preferred approach.

2. *The Question of Domain Expertise*: To make adjustments that are usable, the person performing the planning must have domain expertise with the products and factors related to the products.

CHAPTER 7

Challenges In S&OP Implementation

I have seen, firsthand with S&OP implementations, the difficulties associated with pulling off S&OP are great, and one can't really go into an S&OP project without understanding these challenges because, if you're expecting a project to be easy and it proves difficult, there is a strong tendency to give up. The truth is that S&OP exposes a little-discussed reality of any typical company – the various branches that make up a corporation have competing incentives. To begin, let us outline what these incentives are:

1. *Sales*: Sales is incentivized to increase sales. However, doing things that produce negative externalities on other branches within the company can often increase sales. For example, one of the common problems is that Sales may commit to a customer for a delivery date that cannot be met at current capacity. This may cause inefficiency in the manufacturing process as the production scheduling needs to be moved around, and material expedited to meet an unrealistic goal. This problem gets worse when you realize that, in most companies, sales staff are compensated with a low base salary and

a bonus structure based on sales figures, and that their performance is not benchmarked by profitability, meaning that they have no incentive to avoid increasing costs.

2. *Marketing*: I often combine Marketing with Sales because their incentives are so close; however, they do have a slightly different set of goals. Marketing often demonstrates the value it produces to a company through getting sales from new products, or changing the terms of the sale. One of the most common ways that marketing does this is with promotions. Promotions often increase sales, at least in the short-term, but this leads to all types of unintended consequences, such as altering the sales history (as more is purchased during the promotion and often less purchased after the promotion) and cannibalization of other products that the company may offer. Every new product or promotion they propose, every attempt to justify the investment the company makes in a marketing team, increases the cost of doing business, and makes the job of doing S&OP, demand planning and supply planning more difficult.

3. *Operations*: Operations wants to be able to meet demand with minimal cost. The incentives of operations are generally directly opposed to the incentives of Sales and Marketing. Operations personnel are not compensated based upon sales, and the fewer products a company is featuring, the less change that must be managed and the higher are efficiencies. This may seem like a narrow-minded or backwards way of looking at things, but it is a fact of life. The highest efficiency and quality is produced by companies that have the longest production runs. The highest forecast accuracy is attained from the most stable sales history. The lowest cost on transportation can be attained when the future loads are the most stable.

4. *Finance*: Finance wants to get the most profit from the lowest expenditure. In this way it simply wants the most **predictability** and the lowest variability. They wish to avoid approving investments that do not pay off. Since profitability is a function of how much you sell, selling more is good, but profitability also depends on how much you spend, and any good finance manager knows that costs go down when demand is stable and inventory, production time, and overhead are not wasted.

In addition to the different goals and incentives of each of the major branches, there is also a pecking order. Every company has one, and the pecking order changes depending upon the company. However, in the US at least, the most consistent pecking order that I have witnessed within clients takes the following form:

1. Sales/Marketing

2. Finance

3. Operations

It is quite common for Sales/Marketing to switch places with Finance, but rare for Operations to be anywhere but at the bottom of the order. It was not always this way in the US. In the postwar period, manufacturing and engineering was much more powerful and operations would often take the top position within companies. Generally, operations have a stronger bargaining position when capacity is constrained. In the post-WW2 period in the US, demand tended to outstrip supply, but this condition was historically unusual. Most of the time, supply exceeds demand and, when there is more supply than demand, the natural pressure on any manufacturer is on increasing demand (increasing sales), and, therefore, Sales tends to get priority. A classic and frequently used example of this also comes from the post WW2 period, when General Motors pulled ahead of Ford. They did this, not based upon manufacturing prowess, but because the automotive market in the US had become more or less saturated and, while Ford offered effective, but basic, cars. Under the direction of Alfred P. Sloan, GM enticed consumers with more models, annual changes, step-up models, and newer features – all sales and marketing oriented concepts. Furthermore, money drives behavior, and this preference for Sales/Marketing and Finance positions wound up paying better than Operations, and the power brokers took those jobs preferentially.

Whatever the pecking order within a particular company, it will be the rare company where each of the major branches are **equally matched in influence**. Therefore, the idea, often proposed in books on S&OP, that the S&OP process is where a **meeting of equals** occurs simply does not happen very much in reality. Also note, within each of the major branches are minor branches. For example, operations contain labor specialization and groups in inventory management, manufacturing, quality management, etc. And the influence of these sub-branches affects the major branches. In some companies, inventory management is powerful within Operations. In these cases, the inventory levels tend to be kept low, which impinges upon manufacturing efficiency (more change-overs, less material availability). In other companies, manufacturing is more powerful, and in these companies production runs tend to be longer, and inventory levels kept higher. I have studied the decisions by a number of companies, and I have never seen quantitative justification for choosing one policy versus another – rather, they seem more determined by which groups happen to be the most influential within those companies. All of these orientations cascade up to the major branches and form the bedrock of assumptions that they bring to the S&OP process.

Getting Buy-In

Companies often find it challenging to get the various branches to agree to the S&OP process, as the quote below illustrates.

> *"In many companies, S&OP has become a supply chain process: the process is coordinated by supply chain, all meetings are prepared by supply chain people, and all activities are executed by supply chain. The only involvement of other departments is the presence of the functional managers in the appropriate meeting. Clearly, S&OP will not deliver to its full potential in this situation.*
>
> *Very often, the real problem is not that the sales / marketing / management team does not support the process; the problem is that they don't see the point in supporting it. The reason for that is that nobody actually knows which decisions need to be taken during the S&OP meetings."*
>
> – Sales and Operations Planning, How to
> Avoid the 5 Key Pitfalls

I have witnessed this a number of times myself. There is actually confusion as to what an S&OP meeting is supposed to accomplish. Once, while I sat in with one of my clients at their S&OP meeting, I found that the discussion was nothing more than a supply chain forecasting review meeting, which included the head of forecasting and the demand planners. No one from Sales or Finance was included. Not only is that not an S&OP meeting, it is not even a consensus-based forecast, as it did not include anyone from Sales. I was never able to figure out why they called this meeting an S&OP meeting. Perhaps S&OP was simply a trendy term that they decided to adopt, without following any of the trappings of an S&OP process.

The Politics of the Sales Forecast versus the Supply Chain Forecast

Sales and Operations arrive at their forecasts through very different methods. Operations tends to forecast based upon what it thinks will sell. Sales on the other hand, uses a much more "varied" approach to developing a forecast. For Sales, meeting a forecast determines the compensation for salespeople. Therefore salespeople are in the unusual position of being asked to produce a forecast (which is ostensibly what one thinks will sell), while at the same time, the sales forecast they do produce will be used to determine how they are compensated. When individuals are provided incentives that could lead to their forecast being higher or lower than they actually anticipate, this is referred to as **forecast bias**. The research IT firm, Gartner, provides more insight to this topic. Gartner is on record as stating that sales and marketing input into the S&OP process is one of the lowest quality inputs (and most biased) of the overall S&OP process. How much forecast bias is influenced by institutional demands for bias is an interesting field of study, made even more interesting and perplexing because so little is done to minimize incentives for bias. **The easiest way to remove bias is to remove the institutional incentives for it**. A simple statement to make, but something very rarely done in practice, as many companies have a strong preference against doing so, it falls to the actual forecast process, where adjustments are taken in the demand planning software after biased forecasts have been entered.

Bias Identification

Software designed around the mitigation of forecast bias can help highlight bias and can provide mechanisms for its adjustment. Within the application, there should be the ability to identify bias and the ability to adjust bias quickly and easily. Companies, by and large, do not ask for this, so software companies do not tend to put a lot of focus on bias identification in their software (and do not build bias identification as a main component of the user interface). However, bias identification is important enough that it should have its own dashboard, or view, within all demand planning applications, not only for general ease-of-use but because adjusting for bias is about more than identification and adjustment; it is also about making the case and altering the behavior of the different branches of a company.

According to Charles Chase of SAS, the sales forecast typically has the highest degree of bias and is the least accurate of all forecasting inputs. Bias is the most extreme in sales forecasts, but bias is found to a lesser degree in all forecasting inputs, especially when humans are involved in the generation of said forecasts. For instance, the marketing forecast often has the opposite bias from the sales forecast, as the marketing forecasters have a tendency to think the market opportunities are greater than they are. (Again, salespeople tend to be strongly optimistic, but what they put down as a forecast is strongly influenced by the incentives that are presented to them.) One can see the problem right off the bat. If the sales force is motivated and evaluated on how they exceed the forecast, then they will have an incentive to under-forecast. After all, the best way to achieve one's goal is to make the goal easier to achieve. Operations, on the other hand, **do not strive to exceed the forecast,** because it would mean consumption of safety stock, or a stock outage. Operations hopes the actual sales **are as close to the forecast as possible**.

A forecast is one's estimate of what the demand will be, and it should have no intersection with what one would **like** the demand to be. This would be like asking a person whether or not his or her favorite team will win the game. One can expect a biased response. In fact, forecast bias is introduced into the process simply by the selection of a biased forecaster.

> *Others tell sales people that if they cannot make a forecast they want to hear, the salesperson needs to find another job. They assume that if they allow sales people to tell them anything other than the answer they want to hear, that the sales people will assume they have a license to miss their number. This is not necessarily true and often results in a dangerous situation where the sales reps are only telling management what they want to hear. In situations like these, when*

the sales people can't make their numbers, they say that everything is okay while they line up their next jobs and make excuses for short-term performance ('that deal is just two quarters away…'). This produces a classic 'house of cards' effect in the sales forecast and can be especially catastrophic when there is a dramatic turn or change in the market. Many companies experience huge forecast surprises inthese situations."

— 7 Secrets of Sales Forecasting

I have seen this go quite a ways past simply entering in an incorrect forecasting number to the point where specific prospects are not qualified (that is not questioned regarding their budget -- a basic sales step) in order to allow the prospect who cannot afford the item offered by the company, to continue to be included in the sales forecast.

Generally speaking, forecast accuracy is **not** included in their incentives. In cases where measurements of the forecast accuracy of sales or marketing are taken and discussed (for instance, in consensus forecasting meetings), this measurement rarely has any implication for their compensation or yearly reviews. Therefore, when I analyze the forecasting error at companies, it's quite common for the forecast to have a positive bias. Positive bias can be introduced by either the statistical forecasting system or by the Sales/Marketing input. However, in my forecast error analyses, that bias tends to be greater in Sales and Marketing. The bias of Sales/Marketing in forecasting is so well known that the software vendor Right90 has developed its main application with a focus on managing the bias of sales forecasts. To provide a shorthand explanation, Right90's approach falls into the following steps:

1. *Step 1:* Recognize the historical research on sales forecast bias

2. *Step 2:* Measure forecast bias of each individual providing forecasting input

3. *Step 3:* Control this input:

   a. *Allow Good Input:* Let input with a history of improving the forecast through to change the forecast

    b. *Block Bad Input:* Prevent input with a history of decreasing fore-
       cast accuracy

Another important point to consider is that Sales and Marketing are **not mea-sured** on whether or not they keep inventories low. This is why Sales/Market-ing routinely set unsupportable inventory and service levels. For instance, it is very common for sales groups to target 99 percent service levels for most of its products. However, except for the items with the highest profitability, this service level is not sustainable because the inventory rises so dramatically at service levels above 95 percent (meaning the company is spending too much on stocking inventory to maintain high profit margins). The topic of service levels is covered in *Chapter 8: How Misunderstanding Service Level Undermines Ef-fective S&OP.*

Thirdly, Sales produces forecasts very differently than does Operations. Sales forecasts often have the following characteristics:

1. *Hierarchy of the Forecast*: Produced at a high level in the hierarchy – so at the product family or product group.

2. *The Hierarchy of the Measured Forecast Error*: Operations measures forecast error at the product location combination. However, Sales mea-sures the forecast by dollars and is less concerned with forecast accuracy at the level of Operations. This brings up an amusing quotation which I heard second hand at one of my clients, a quotation stated by the head of Sales: "*I don't understand why we stock-out. If you look at the forecast accuracy of sales, it's high! However, we still don't have the right products when the customer demand arrives.*" Sales forecast accuracy is typically measured as revenue. Therefore, if Sales forecasts one million dollars in sales, and $900,000 is sold, the forecast is 90 percent accurate. But what does that say about the accuracy of the individual product location forecast, which is how Operations must measure its forecast accuracy? It says absolutely nothing.

3. *Location of the Forecast*: Produced by a customer or per a customer lo-cation rather than the supply chain forecast which is produced at the stocking location.

4. *The Use of CRM*: Sales will often forecast in their CRM system rather than using the same system used by Operations. A major problem is that CRM is **not designed** to track the sales at a product-location combination. Instead, the unit of measure of CRM applications tends to be sales and the focus is on the customer. While CRM was never developed for forecasting, it is often presumed that it is used for forecasting. In fact, many CRM software vendors propose that their system is the key to improving the accuracy of the sales forecast. CRM is focused almost exclusively on revenue tracking and revenue forecasting rather than forecasting a particular product-location combination.

5. *Market Intelligence*: Much is emphasized within companies regarding the market intelligence that salespeople bring to forecast, however, few companies provide salespeople with either the time or the training to properly convert this market intelligence into forecast adjustments.

The fact that there are so many differences between the Sales forecast and the forecast produced by Operations, means there are frequent challenges in getting a final/unified forecast between Sales and Operations even without consideration for the S&OP process.

The way Sales performs its planning is actually much closer to the standard or traditional way that S&OP is performed.

> *"The S&OP process is generally carried out at an aggregate level, often at product family. This enables the S&OP process to be agile, focusing on enabling aligned decision-making rather than granular precision. The S&OP process should incorporate scenario planning and contingency planning, allowing considered trade-off decisions to be made. On its own, the S&OP process doesn't offer an end to end solution to planning. It needs to be integrated correctly into the broader planning framework."*
>
> – The Planning Blog

Interpretation and Planning of Consensus Planning Processes

S&OP is a consensus planning process. However, there is already plenty of experience with consensus planning processes. The real story about consen-

sus-planning processes is considerably more complicated. In fact, consensus-planning processes are very much a process of receiving input and then
performing analytical filtering to remove or reduce the impact of individuals
or groups with poor forecasting accuracy. This part of consensus-planning
processes is under emphasized, probably because it's not as appealing as the
story of simply increasing participation. The next logical question is, *"Who is
going to get their input reduced?"* which then begs the question of how this
topic is raised during the implementation of consensus-planning processes
projects.

What we now consider consensus based forecasting was first formally studied at the RAND Institute and the approach that RAND developed was
called the Delphi Method. This project was named after the city of Delphi in
Greece, the location of the Oracles who were consulted by the Ancient Greeks
and Romans among many others. The Delphi Method is now just one method of consensus based forecasting. RAND's research into the Delphi Method
goes back to 1943 and they performed a number of studies on this topic.
The original intent of the research was to obtain better group judgment, for
example, by performing research into how the effect of strong personality
types on groups can be mitigated (the research had the participants isolated
from one another). Since then, consensus based planning methods have been
studied in a number ways and applied to a wide variety of disciplines. The
majority of academic research in consensus based forecasting is outside of
supply chain management and is concentrated in areas such as finance and,
specifically, trading. However, S&OP is not the Delphi Method, as the Delphi
Method is a remote approach with structured rules to control for too much
influence coming from any one participant. This combined with the common feature within companies for certain branches to have more political
power than others means that S&OP is quite susceptible to overwhelming
influence coming from the stronger participants. This observation goes vir-
tually unmentioned in the general literature on S&OP. That is even though
the evidence is clear that consensus based methods where each individual's
input is publicly known, that this leads to some individuals exercising disproportionate influence on the overall output, S&OP literature tends to not
acknowledge this.

New S&OP?

Another strong bias of publications and conferences is to present all ideas as new, and the more revolutionary the better. So for example, ERP systems were going to integrate companies so there would not be islands that didn't communicate with one another, new business intelligence were going to allow companies to see patterns that they had never seen before, allow research entities to cure diseases and so on.

In the years I have spent in information technology most of the enterprise software forecasts have **overstated** that actual change that they produced. And it should be recognized that there are never any apologies. The marketing departments of vendors or of consulting companies that make false projections in the past will continue to make false projections in the future. There have been some information technologies that over performed expectations, however, they have not been in enterprise software, but instead in technologies such as GPS and mobile phones. But in enterprise software the clear pattern is one of overstatement.

If we turn our attention to the topic of a bias for newness, or presenting things as if they are completely new, it is quite logical that people trying to accomplish goals since as long people started coordinating to accomplish things have held S&OP meetings. If we think about building the pyramids, someone had to **forecast** how many cut slabs of stone could be placed upon the pyramid (the demand) and this forecast had to be used to **plan** how many people would be cutting the slabs, the capacity of the barge that carried the slab up the Nile (the supply), and the person financing the operation needed to determine how much funding they had to allow for this many workers, this many barges, etc. (the financial plan). That is the heart of the S&OP process. They may have been performing the calculations on scrolls, rather than using a software application, but S&OP is a process, which is **independent of a technology**. Up until recently S&OP has been facilitated with spreadsheets, more recently specialized applications have arisen to support the process, who knows what will be used in the distant future? All of this is to say that while S&OP is a recently derived term, the process it describes is not new. And secondly, the S&OP process has always been subject to politics different agendas, and until humans are replaced by perfectly logical androids, it always will be.

The Increased Complexity of Planning

What has changed is that S&OP is more complicated than before, which is true of planning generally. Most books and articles on the topic tend to portray things like shorter product life cycles, more new product introductions more promotions with a slightly positive tinge, and as if these features are simply unalterable factors of the marketplace. However, these are actually optional things (or should I say self inflicted) that have been done to increase the complexity of operating businesses, and there is little actual evidence that this increased complexity improves profitability. However, the changes are quite significant. Lets take a look at two items that have significantly increased planning complexity: promotions and product proliferation.

Promotions

Promotions are a complexity that is modeled by Marketing and in the S&OP process as well. A promotion essentially alters the terms of the sale (promotions can be wholesale or retail). According to Gartner; roughly 20 percent of the revenue of manufacturers is spent on promotions, up from **.5 percent in 1985**.[1] For many consumer packaged goods companies, promotions are now the majority of their overall advertising expense.[2] Promotions are stated as being significant drivers of profitability by marketing, but what is their actual effect in this regards? What is the evidence regarding promotions and sales and profitability? Considering the popularity of promotions, the evidence for them is quite mixed, and non-sales and non-marketing executives often take it for granted that the benefits of promotions are quite substantial. However, once one looks at the actual research into promotions, the benefits seems far less clear than assumed.

> *"So do price promotions pay off? To answer that question, we
> analyzed seven years of scanner data, covering 25 product categories
> and 75 brands, from the Chicago area's second-largest supermarket
> chain, Dominick's Finer Foods. Previous research showed that price*

---

[1] Hagemeyer, Dale. Vendor Panorama for Trade Promotion Management in Consumer Goods. Gartner, 2012.

[2] Lucas, Anthony. "In-Store Trade Promotions – Profit or Loss?" Journal of Consumer Marketing. April 1, 1996.

promotions tend to have little long-term effect on sales volume. Our
new research found that the same is true for revenues and margins:
They quickly snap back to baseline. But in the short-to-medium-term,
promotions can have very strong positive and negative effects that can
hit retailers and manufacturers in very different ways."

           – Who Benefits from Price Promotions?

Companies that perform promotions often lose track of the effect of promotions, which means that the companies most often lack an understanding of the relationship between future promotions and the actual impact on demand of the promoted item or of other items that are affected by promotion but are not promoted themselves. A relatively new category of enterprise software called Trade Promotion Management is designed to help companies better manage their promotions, but only a minority of companies use a TPM application and there are many questions to be answered in terms of how the TPM information comes across to the demand planning system and ends up driving the forecast.

Product Proliferation

Product proliferation is the increase in the number of products that are carried. Often the marketing differences between the products are only incidental and illusory. An excellent example of product proliferation is toothpaste.

Most of these toothpaste containers essentially contain a similar set of chemical com-
pounds; however, marketing provides customers with different varieties of what is of-

ten the same product in order to promote purchases. Many of the claims are unfounded, but because there is very little regulation (in the US at least), they can say what they like regarding what the toothpaste will do for consumers.

Proliferation would be even worse than it currently is, but retailers only have so much space to offer. There may be no better example of an industry that has gone to the extreme with unnecessary product proliferation as the grocery industry. The typical U.S. grocery store has between 35,000 and 50,000 SKUs, which is a massive increase in SKUs over the past several decades. When standing, one can no longer see over most grocery store shelves. However, one grocery chain takes a different path, and this is a major reason they perform so much better than the industry average. I covered Trader Joe's in the SCM Focus Press book *Supply Chain Forecasting Software*. Introducing a high number of new products is supposed to drive increased profitability, but does it? The conclusion of the book *Islands of Profit in a Sea of Red Ink* is that it generally doesn't.

> *"Nearly every company is 30 to 40 percent unprofitable by any measure. In almost every company 20 to 30 percent of the business is highly profitable, and a large proportion of this profitability is going to cross-subsidize the unprofitable part of the business. The rest of the company is marginal. The most current metrics and control systems (budgets, etc.) do not even show the problem or the opportunity for improvement."*

> *"Some managers argue that it is a good idea to accept business that contributes, even marginally, to covering overhead. However, when you take on a lot of business that contributes only marginally to overhead, in almost all cases it will absorb a significant amount of sales and operations resources that otherwise would have been devoted to increasing your "good" business. And it will remain and grow into the embedded profitability that drags down earnings in company after company.*

> *"If the underlying reason for taking marginal business is to fill unused capacity, you need a sunset policy to stop taking the marginal*

business once capacity is filled and to remove it when full freight business is available. Not many companies have the information and discipline to do this."

– Islands of Profit in a Sea of Red Ink

How Product Proliferation Interferes with Manufacturing and Supply Chain Productivity

Spreading the same sales over more products (or services as the same thing has happened to services although to a lesser degree) means more resources to manage. Unrealized by many, creating fewer products with longer production runs, which are sold at stable prices, is a very efficient and productive environment, and an environment which is much easier to plan than the converse. The same is true of the supply network. The fewer stocking locations given a stable sales level, the more demand is applied to each stocking location and the faster that stocking location will turn over, and the easier it will be to manage at a high service level with lower inventory costs.

In manufacturing, for all the talk of "flexible manufacturing" (a term most popular with those that have the least experience in manufacturing), the costs associated with manufacturing changeovers have not changed very much. Most of the improvement in manufacturing has not come from making manufacturing more flexible (or moving more to job shop), but from moving manufacturing facilities to very low cost countries, where the flexibility is not any higher, but the costs of manufacturing are so low that changeover costs are less relevant, as manufacturing costs overall are less relevant. After manufacturing, the costs of maintaining more stock keeping units (SKUs) is more inventory being carried and more inventory obsolescence. Technology can reduce these costs by some degree – for instance, using more advanced software that repositions stock to locations where it is more likely to be consumed. Software called multi echelon and inventory optimization is the best at repositioning or "redeploying" stock – although few companies can actually pull off software of this level of complexity. However, a company with more or increasingly many more products, more new products, and more promotions – for a given sales level is going to also have more planning overhead. Does this make S&OP more necessary than ever before? That point is debatable, however, it certainly makes the S&OP process, along with every other planning process more challenging.

This is not to say that there is any stopping these changes. People reading this book will need to play the hand they are dealt and, in most cases, this means an unnecessary degree of complexity in the supply chain. However, many of the articles that purport to declare the increased importance of S&OP are based on little evidence, and assume that all changes that have occurred that make planning processes complex over the past several decades are if not good, at least certainly not bad.

Conclusion

The political challenges of pulling off successful S&OP are greatly underestimated in the literature. The reason for this difficulty is that S&OP jumps right into the areas where the branches within a company meet, and each branch has a different set of incentives. These incentives change very little from company to company, and we have discussed them in detail. Each group has different things that they want, with Sales/Marketing and Operations being particularly divergent from one another. The policy of the company is determined by the interaction of these branches of the company, with the resulting policy having much less to do with something that is quantitatively proven, and more to do which with group ends up getting its way. The more powerful one branch is versus the others, the less the S&OP process can add value by exposing the trade-offs that are inherent in different choices. Within each of the major branches that are listed as participating in S&OP, there are minor branches which exert their influence in proportion to their position in the company. A company may decide to keep very low inventories, leading to shorter production runs, simply because manufacturing happens to be more influential in that company that materials management. When the production and inventory plan is brought into the S&OP application or spreadsheet, these predispositions transfer along with the plan. The power and influence of Sales/ Marketing has made both supply chain planning and S&OP more complex that it would ordinarily be. It means planning for more products, more promotions, more "one offs" more discussions of customer prioritization, etc.

The applications that can be used for S&OP keep improving and becoming more powerful, however S&OP, as a process, is not new. The long-term balancing of supply and demand along with the calculation of budgets in order to support a given level of demand has been a universal need for any entity trying to accomplish an objective. A

military is not selling a product, but war planners have had to consider attack or defense plans and then how to fund these plans since the first military action occurred.

CHAPTER 8

How Misunderstanding Service Level Undermines Effective S&OP

Safety stock is set in a variety of ways in companies. It is often set by judgment methods, like manual approximation or with averaging – such as with day's supply - or with more complex formulae like dynamic safety stock. In this chapter, I will cover all of the commonly used ways of setting safety stock that I have come across in my consulting experience and provide an explanation of how each method is used and its effectiveness. This will then be correlated to the effect on service level.

Manual Approximation

Safety stock is often set in companies by simply allowing individuals to guesstimate what the safety stock value should be and then providing them with the rights to make the safety stock adjustments. Sometimes, the manual approximation is performed with the broader interests of the product location database in mind, but often manual approximation is performed by an individual with a bias towards a particular item or a particular group of items.

How Manual Approximation Works in Practice

I have never seen manual approximation work very well – and one of the primary reasons for this is that the person making these manual changes most often does not understand how safety stock fits into inventory management. I have witnessed safety stock being set by individuals in Sales. However, Sales has a bias to maintain more inventory than Supply Chain does because they want to set the inventory at a level that maximizes sales. Secondly, Sales tends to not have a global view.

Firstly, salespeople are generally not aware of how much it costs to maintain inventory, nor are they held accountable for the inventory level. However, they are compensated on their sales revenue, which in turn depends upon having the time to sell – so Sales has a strong bias to increase inventory whenever possible.

Secondly, there is a great deal of competition between salespeople, so Sales is really a group of competing individuals that are managed by a central overseer. That is, if one salesperson is responsible for selling some items, they may simply increase the safety stock for their items and not worry about how this affects the stocking levels of other items. Companies only have so much money to put into inventory, so if they over-allocate inventory to one set of (product location combinations) PLCs, they must under-allocate to other PLCs. However, salespeople normally only consider how the inventory levels that are set affect "their products."

I believe the reason that planners and other supply chain planning professionals tend to focus on safety stock is not because of formal training or reading about the topic, but because it is one of the few inventory values easily altered in almost all supply planning systems. Absent a foundational understanding of the topic, people have a strong tendency to base their views on what they can control.

This is reminiscent of the story about the man who was looking in the street for his keys one night. When asked where he lost them, he replied, "On the other side of the street." Why was he looking on the wrong side of the street? Because "the light is better over here."

In the same way, even though safety stock is not a good inventory value to adjust manually, it is frequently adjusted simply because it is a convenient way of controlling the stock level within many systems. This causes problems, as safety stock is simply the portion of overall stock allocated specifically to variability.

Stock levels should **not be** controlled by manually adjusting the safety stock. Instead, safety stock should be dynamically calculated and automated, and only changed as a result of changes in the variability of supply or demand. When this is done, it is called "dynamic safety stock," and this functionality is now common in both ERP and APS systems. The standard safety stock formula resolves part of the problem; but it is an incomplete solution, as will be explained in detail further on in the book.

Even though there is ample evidence that allowing manual approximation of safety stock does not lead to good inventory and service level outcomes, it continues to be a very common way to set safety stock. A primary reason for this is that many companies don't feel as if there is a "right answer" when it comes to safety stock. However, there are far better ways to set it; they just may not happen to be some of the common ways that are explained to people.

Day's Supply Combined With a Fixed Value
Currently the most commonly used and successful way of setting safety stock is to use a combination of a day's supply combined with a fixed value.

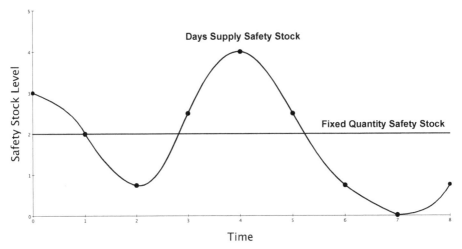

This approach works well because it varies, an important criterion for safety stock, but it does so in a way that is relatively easy to set. Essentially, this is a minimum/maximum way of setting safety stock. The day's supply value is the maximum. This changes with the forecast. So if the forecast is 100 units for a week, and the day's supply is 3 days, then the safety stock value would be 3/7 * 100 or 42.85, rounded to 43 units.

However, due to the downward variability in some forecasts, day's supply will not work by itself; this is why blending it with a lower set value prevents the safety stock from dropping too low. However, with the upper level taken care of by day's supply, not a great deal of effort is required to calculate the minimum value.

Days' Supply Safety Stock Calculator

		Setting	Mon	Tue	Wed	Thur	Fri	Sat	Sun	Mon	Tue	Wed
	Forecast		25	10	2	0	5	5	35	45	40	65
A	Days' Supply Calculation	3 Days	37	12	7	10	45	85	120	150		
B	Minimum Safety Stock	20	20	20	20	20	20	20	20	20	20	20
	Resulting Safety Stock	Max(A,B)	37	20	20	20	45	85	120			

Here is an example of how day's supply works in detail. Along the time horizon that is represented in the image above, this is the 3-day forward-looking day's supply safety stock calculation.

The Resulting Safety Stock value simply takes the maximum of the Day's Supply Calculation and the Minimum Safety Stock. During periods of average to high forecasts, the Day's Supply Calculation ends up setting the safety stock. However on the black periods, when the forecast is low, the Minimum Safety Stock sets the actual Resulting Safety Stock value.

Therefore, the company can meet the demand in the average to high periods and also keep enough safety stock when the forecast dissipates. Safety stock should not perfectly track with the forecast, because safety stock is a buffer, and the forecast, as well as the supply, has variability or error.

This is a standard functionality in many ERP systems. However, I have actually seen the functionality decline when one moves from ERP to an advanced planning system. This is explained in the following quotation from SCM Focus on the topic of using the SNP optimizer for a client that moved from the far less sophisticated SAP ECC ERP system:

> *The SM (combined safety stock day's supply and minimum safety stock value) Safety Stock Method does not work with the optimizer. This means that companies that currently use the optimizer must understand that they must use either the Safety Stock that is hard-coded into the Material Master or the Safety Time, but the system* ***will not use either of the two.***
>
> *The way to approach this is to set only the Safety Stock quantity or the Days of Supply. If only the Safety Stock quantity is entered into the Material Master then the Safety Stock Method will change to SB, while if only the Days of Supply is used then the Safety Stock Method in APO becomes SZ. This would mean using the mass maintenance transaction to change every location/product combination in ERP to hold only a Safety Stock Quantity or a Days Supply.*
>
> *However, there is more to this than simply the master data change. When analyzing this for one project it was working on, it was brought up that the current Safety Stock Quantities had been setup on the low side because they were designed really only to protect the lower*

end of the range, and essentially the Safety Stock Quantities were developed to work with the Days of Supply, or designed to work with the SM Safety Stock Method. Once Days of Supply is taken out of the equation for certain Location Products, which the Safety Stock Quantity would have to be increased. This of course requires that the business go through and increase these Safety Stock Quantities to the appropriate levels if the Days of Supply is never used.

How Day's Supply With Fixed Value Works in Practice

This approach works very well for many companies because it accounts for variability but also prevents the safety stock from falling away during periods of low demand. This method lacks sophistication and is significantly less desirable than the method of setting safety stock that will be described in Chapter 8.However it is, I believe, the most successful broadly-used approach to safety stock setting.

The Dynamic Safety Stock

The basic concept of the dynamic safety stock calculation is to adjust the safety stock per multiple factors. Often the explanation of dynamic safety stock is that it is to adjust for both supply and demand variability - as is expressed in the graphic below:

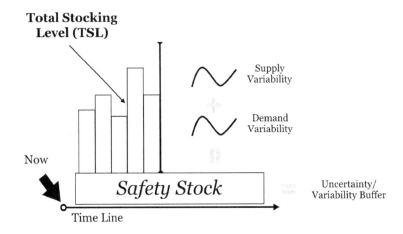

This is the dynamic safety stock formula:

Safety Stock: {Z*SQRT(Avg. Lead-time*Standard Deviation of Demand^2 + Avg. Demand^2*Standard Deviation of Lead-time^2}

This formula multiplies the average lead-time by the squared standard deviation of demand. It then takes the squared average demand and multiplies it by the squared standard deviation of lead-time. It then contains the following components:

1. *The Square Root Component:* Take the square root of the product of the primary values.

2. *The Service Level Component:* Multiply this value by "Z" which is the number of standard deviations above the mean that are determined by the inverse of the normal distribution of the service level.

This calculation is straightforward until one gets to step 2, which is the service level component. The reason for this is explained below.

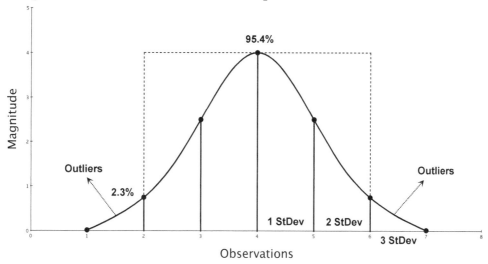

Let's start off with the normal distribution. Now safety stock can actually be based upon any probability distribution, but it is normally based upon the normal distribution. The logic is that the variance will be normally distributed. If the errors are not normally distributed, for instance in the case of service parts, then another probability distribution should be used. However, let's begin by reviewing the normal distribution above. You can see that 95.4% of the values would fall within two standard deviations

*of the mean. However, this leaves areas on **both sides of the normal distribution uncovered** - and we want to cover all the possible options, all the way up to the second standard deviation to the right of the mean. Therefore the actual values we want to cover by setting the safety stock are the following:*

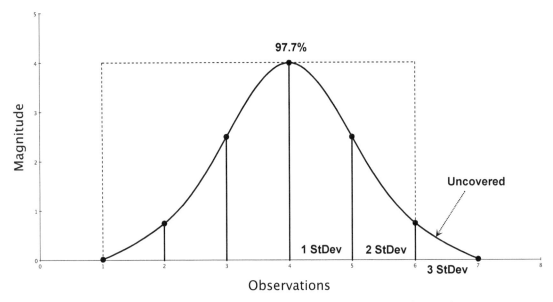

*By covering everything up to the second standard deviation up from the mean, we end up covering **97.7%** of the predicted possible occurrences. The graphic above is **not a** high-detail graph, because there are more standard deviations above the second standard deviation.*

*For instance, three standard deviations to the right of the mean covers **99.9%** of all of the predicted occurrences. This level of service is never attained in supply chain management. Therefore, the service level can be converted into a standard deviation, which can then be used to multiply the values that result from step 2 in the formula steps listed above. If the desired service level is **96%**, then the standard deviation to use the safety stock formula is 1.75. A desired service level of 98% would use a standard deviation of 2.05 in step 3 of the safety stock formula.*

When people write about dynamic safety stock, they tend to not discuss the validity of the formula, but instead tend to quickly discuss its features. For instance, they point out that the dynamic safety stock calculation adjusts across the dimensions of service level, lead-time, and forecast error both in variability (in terms of lead-time and forecast error) as well as lead-time duration. This formula can be used to model the inventory and supply chain of an entire company. That is, instead of entering the values for a single SKU, the overall or average values can be used to help see the relationships between things like service level and the total amount of stock carried. The dynamic safety stock formula has been around for quite some time and has been incorporated into many applications with supply planning functionality. However, what is very rarely discussed is how dynamic safety stock actually works when deployed in a company.

How Dynamic Safety Stock Works in Practice

The easiest part of dynamic safety stock to understand is the service level or Z value. This is simply a probability multiplier, which assumes a normal distribution of occurrences. However, the rest of the formula is much less understandable. The following questions should be asked:

1. Why is it correct to square the values that are squared?

2. Why should the lead-time be multiplied by the forecast error or standard deviation of demand and vice versa?

The formula seems appropriately authoritative, but the more time I have spent working with the formula, the less the formula has made any sense to me. One of my major issues with those that propose the use of the standard dynamic safety stock formula is the assumption often made that the formula has been **proven in industry**, where the primary evidence for this is that the formula has been around for a long time.

However, the reality is just the opposite. The formula is little used in industry, and I could find no research papers that even tested whether the standard dynamic safety stock formula was used **or broadly successful**. I can say from my consulting experience that it is generally unused, although companies often attempt to use it. They often read about the benefits of the standard dynamic safety stock formula in a book or from a consultant, neither of which may have ever extensively tested the formula.

They then learn that the standard dynamic safety stock formula is **already available** within their supply planning application. But companies are normally unaware that few successful implementations of the dynamic safety stock formula exist. Very quickly the conversation moves to how great it would be to implement the dynamic safety stock, and the formula also provides the company with the feeling that they are moving to the leading edge by implementing this approach.

In investigating this formula, I found that explanation of dynamic safety stock is difficult to obtain. Upon review of the available safety stock calculation spreadsheets available from the Internet, I found all of them to be seriously deficient in **not fully explaining** the formula. Almost every one of the calculators asked for a service level input, but did not even explain the definition of the service level calculation definition to be used. How any person is supposed to use the online calculator reliably without knowing the correct units of measure to use is beyond me.

The vast majority of these online calculators **ignored** the lead-time component of the formula and only provided input for sales/forecast variability (error). This is **not a good way** to explain how dynamic safety stock works. Interestingly, those that left out part of formula did not even explain that it was left out - giving any person who is trying to understand the entire formula a problem. It seems as if many people want to talk about dynamic safety stock, but essentially **no one** was interested in making a clear calculator that explains safety stock.

Furthermore, there is a broader problem with the formula in that most of the explanations are not specific enough as to what the author or creator is referring to. For instance, what is "Average Demand?" Without knowing the duration that applies to the average demand, this does not mean very much. Is this the average over lead-time? The monthly average? The yearly average? Various online safety stock calculators are available at SCM Focus at the following link.

http://www.scmfocus.com/supplyplanning/2014/04/08/safety-stock-calculator/

A reverse safety stock calculator is also available at this link.

http://www.scmfocus.com/supplyplanning/2014/04/10/reverse-dynamic-safety-stock-calculation/

Conclusion

From my consulting experience, I have concluded that there is clearly a major opportunity with respect to safety stock within companies. None of the common approaches used (Manual Approximation, Days' Supply Combined with a Fixed Value, Dynamic Safety Stock, etc.) are particularly good at managing safety stock.

Of the current methods, the day's supply with fixed value approach, which is the most effective that I have seen used, is still substantially inferior to a safety stock calculation method that takes into consideration much more than simply demand combined with a lower limit to prevent the safety stock from declining too significantly when demand declines. Although there is nothing to prevent the days' supply method from being used along with an external calculator. This is where the minimum safety stock is set by the external calculator and the upper limit is set by the days' supply.

What this means for S&OP is that for applications that use the safety stock of the ERP system or advanced planning system, there is most likely a great deal of inaccuracy with respect to the safety stock values (which are incorporated into the overall stocking level." For S&OP applications that calculate the safety stock internally, there is a stronger ability to simulate changes to service level and stocking level, but then the particular method used in the S&OP application must be fully evaluated and then correlated to how safety stock is set in the ERP or planning systems.

Conclusion

S&OP is an important, but often underused, process. It is designed to connect the business by connecting all the different branches and by merging the top-level strategic planning with the operational planning. S&OP has much less structure in companies than do lower-level planning activities such as supply planning or shorter term budget planning, and the software industry has been much slower to develop and market S&OP applications versus lower-level planning applications.

The overlap between S&OP applications, spreadsheets and other low-level planning tools lower-level is very important, because an S&OP design will mean following a particular process that will mean performing some processing and sending some data from lower-level planning systems to the S&OP system. Any application that is purchased should match the way that the company wants to perform S&OP, and not all S&OP applications have the same design. Options include having full resource visibility in the S&OP system, reproducing the supply and production plan using a procedure in S&OP, or instead receiving an already finalized supply and production plan from lower-level planning systems. These are just a few examples and the options are really quite numerous.

The S&OP literature has a strong bias in focusing on manufacturing companies; however, S&OP is not any less relevant outside of manufacturing. Not only do service industries require an S&OP process, but government entities also have needs for S&OP. For these entities, there is really very little literature available to them, and the best option is to simply adopt S&OP practices from the literature on S&OP on manufacturing. In terms of software, I am unaware of S&OP software that can be used for companies that are not distributing some type of product. However, even most manufacturing companies are still using spreadsheets rather than dedicated S&OP applications, non-manufacturing companies can simply develop their own custom S&OP spreadsheets, which at some level, most probably have.

In the standard S&OP process, there is a review and sign off for three basic steps:

1. Review and Sign Off on the Demand Plan

2. Review and Sign Off on the Supply Plan

3. Review and Sign Off on the Financial Plan

Now within each of these major process steps, there is a lot of room for variance in terms of how each company performs these steps.

The data that is sent to S&OP systems has been processed by specialists, so an open question is how much time should be spent modifying these plans. And if they are modified, how to get the modifications back to the lower-level planning systems, as this is where the plans are actually generated. S&OP is more of an offline process, while the lower-level planning systems are on-line and connected to live/production systems. Some of the outputs of the S&OP process will mean making changes to lower-level planning systems in terms of things like planned orders or purchase requisitions, what is known as transactions. However, other changes are related to capacity, such as approving new manufacturing line to be created, which will mean planning the acquisition of new machines, the hiring of more people, etc.

While it can sometime sound like it there is not necessarily a single S&OP process within companies. S&OP can be performed for different regions before being rolled into a global S&OP process. Connecting all of these different S&OP processes is tricky. It means bringing in data feeds from applications that may be hosted all over the world, and then reconciling this data in single system, which then simply allows different views to be seen within the application. This is the **best possible scenario**. Often different national or regional groups will have their own applications, or more often their own spreadsheets, and in this case the process of reconciliation is very time consuming and error prone. For companies that have global needs for S&OP a single application is preferable, but creating a global instance of planning applications is also tricky, as each regional group will often propose that it has its own specific requirements and want to setup the system their own way. For example, for a multinational, one country may do all the manufacturing, while the other only distributes the products into a country. In this case these two countries within the multinational will have different requirements and may not be able to agree how to configure the application. With multiple geographic S&OP processes, any company with this requirement has be very careful in the application that they purchase it must meet the requirement of different geographies and it must be worked out how all of these S&OP planning results will coalesce into a unified view. As S&OP grows in popularity and scales in complexity, companies will find that they need to hire more staff to support the process and the S&OP application. Reviewing the open job listings on job websites, I did find some of these roles, but not nearly as many as I would have expected. I am personally being asked about my S&OP knowledge more than I ever recall being asked before.

S&OP is an aggregated planning process, however, the proper level of aggregation must be selected, and this in turn brings up question as to what degree feasibility can be determined. A related question for S&OP is how the S&OP application and process will overlap with the supply chain planning application or process. There is much to work out here, and the first question is what application is doing what and why. I can see in a number of S&OP applications that functionalities are demonstrated, but companies often do not think though the interactions with lower-level planning systems. This leads to another important point that if adjustments are being made in the S&OP system that will be incorporated into the planning system, then are these adjustments made by those with domain expertise required to make the adjustment. Once the adjustment is made how are the people that plan full time supposed to incorporate these adjustments into their plan? What if they disagree with the adjustments and consider them unrealistic of if they are not actually feasible?

S&OP means bringing together the major branches within the company to agree on planning. However, each of the branches, in addition to the sub-branches within each branch has very different incentives, which will preclude them from seeing things the same way. Secondly, many entities find that the different branches tend to buy into S&OP to different degrees. While the S&OP literature tends to talk up how S&OP is a universal virtue – essentially relying upon the assumption that everyone wants to participate, there are in many companies where a least some of the branches prefer to "do their own thing." Of course doing one's own thing leads to conflict down the road when there is not the capacity to meet demand, or when one group is criticized for not "reading the mind" of the other branch. It may seem illogical, but the fact is that getting buy-in from all the groups, including getting their participation is a well-known issue.

S&OP is a consensus based process, and consensus based processes have been extensively studied. A consensus-based process, particularly when it is among individuals/entities with different incentives, must deal with conflict. Somewhere along the way, one of the participants is going to have their input reduced. The Delphi Method was developed to stop the common feature of collaborative-based processes where the strongest or most forceful entity ends up overwhelming the other participants. However, S&OP is not the Delphi Method, as the Delphi Method is a remote approach with structured rules to control for too much influence coming from any one participant.

S&OP is a process, which is necessary, but still so often inadequately performed. It has complexity related to its integration with other planning processes, how regional S&OP processes mesh with higher-level S&OP processes, and is one of the most political planning processes that entities engage it. One way or another, in isolation or in collaboration, these decisions will be made. The question is not getting to a perfect state, but how much the current state can be improved. This is best facilitated by understanding all of the challenges that are presented to performing an effective S&OP process, and analyzing the available approaches and tools that can be used to make as much improvement as is possible.

References

Byrnes, Jonathan. Islands of Profit in a Sea of Red Ink. Portfolio Hardcover. 2010.

Few, Stephen. *Now You See It: Simple Visualization Techniques for Quantitative Analysis.* Analytics Press, 2009.

Guido Grüne, Stephanie Lockemann, Volker Kluy. Business Process Management within Chemical and Pharmaceutical Industries. Springer Press. 2013

Hagemeyer,Dale. *Vendor Panorama for Trade Promotion Management in Consumer Goods.*Gartner, 2012.

Integrated Business Planning
Wikipedia, October 15 2015
https://en.wikipedia.org/wiki/Integrated_business_planning

Lucas, Anthony. "In-Store Trade Promotions – Profit or Loss?" *Journal of Consumer Marketing.* April 1, 1996.

Olhager, Jan. Rudgerg, Martin. Wikner, Joakim. Long-term Capacity Management: Linking the Perspectives from Manufacturing Strategy and Sales Operations Planning. International Journal of Production Economics. 2001.

Right90. *7 Secrets of Sales Forecasting.*
http://www.right90.com/whitepapers/7_secrets_of_sales_forecastingFINALPRINT.pdf.

"Stahley, Tim. *From Misery to Mastery: How to Build a Better Sales Forecast.*
http://www.right90.com/whitepapers/Misery_to_Mastery_White%20
Paper_10_14NOCHANGES.pdf.

Snapp, Shaun. Forecast Parameters: Alpha, Beta Gamma, etc..SCM Focus Press. 2014.

Snapp, Shaun. Superplant: Creating a Nimble Manufacturing Enterprise with Adaptive Planning Software.SCM Focus Press. 2013.

Snapp, Shaun. Inventory Optimization and Multi Echelon Software.SCM Focus Press. 2012.

Snapp, Shaun. *Inventory Optimization and Multi-Echelon Planning Software.* SCM Focus Press, 2012.

Snapp, Shaun. Constrained Supply and Production Planning in SAP APO.SCM Focus Press. 2013.

Snapp, Shaun. Replenishment Triggers: Setting Systems for Make to Stock, Make to Order & Assemble to Order. SCM Focus Press. 2015.

Sales and Operations Planning, October 9 2015
https://en.wikipedia.org/wiki/Sales_and_operations_planning

Wacker, G John.Lummus, Ronda R. Sales Forecasting for Strategic Resource Planning. International Journal of Operations and Production Management. 2002.

http://www.nytimes.com/2013/01/23/us/unfinished-tower-in-las-vegas-is-symbol-of-a-reversal.html

http://www.reviewjournal.com/columns-blogs/inside-gaming/macau-free-fall-and-taking-wynn-resorts-it

http://thetaylorreachgroup.com/2012/04/26/why-most-call-center-customer-service-is-so-bad/

http://www.helpscout.net/75-customer-service-facts-quotes-statistics/

http://www.teslamotors.com/gigafactory

http://www.forbes.com/sites/stevebanker/2015/07/16/sales-operations-planning-continues-to-evolve/

http://www.boozallen.com/media/file/Lessons_From_The_Shop_Floor.pdf

http://theplanningblog.com/integrating-the-sop-process-go-with-the-flow/

http://clarkstonconsulting.com/wp-content/uploads/2015/04/IBP_SupplyChain.pdf

https://www.youtube.com/watch?v=h4tbejP4rkE

http://www.mobiusuk.co.uk/articles/2012/11/16/sales-and-operations-planning-how-to-avoid-the-5-key-pitfalls/

https://www.sapstore.com/solutions/60032/SAP-Integrated-Business-Planning-for-sales-and-operations

Author Profile

Shaun Snapp is the founder and editor of SCM Focus. SCM Focus is one of the largest independent
supply chain software analysis and educational
sites on the Internet.

After working at several of the largest consulting
companies and at i2 Technologies, he became an
independent consultant and later started SCM Focus. He maintains a strong interest in comparative
software design, and works both in SAP APO as
well as with a variety of best-of-breed supply chain
planning vendors. His ongoing relationships with these vendors
keep him on the cutting edge of emerging technology.

Primary Sources of Information and Writing Topics

Shaun writes about topics with which he has firsthand experience.
These topics range from recovering problematic implementations,
to system configuration, to socializing complex software and supply
chain concepts in the areas of demand planning, supply planning
and production planning.

More broadly, he writes on topics supportive of these applications, which include master data parameter management, integration, analytics, simulation and bill of material management systems. He covers management aspects of enterprise software ranging from software policy to handling consulting partners on SAP projects.

Shaun writes from an implementer's perspective and as a result he focuses on how software is actually used in practice rather than its hypothetical or "pure release note capabilities." Unlike many authors in enterprise software who keep their distance from discussing the realities of software implementation, he writes both on the problems as well as the successes of his software use. This gives him a distinctive voice in the field.

Secondary Sources of Information

In addition to project experience, Shaun's interest in academic literature is a secondary source of information for his books and articles. Intrigued with the historical perspective of supply chain software, much of his writing is influenced by his readings and research into how different categories of supply chain software developed, evolved, and finally became broadly used over time.

Covering the Latest Software Developments

Shaun is focused on supply chain software selections and implementation improvement through writing and consulting, bringing companies some of the newest technologies and methods. Some of the software developments that Shaun showcases at SCM Focus and in books at SCM Focus Press have yet to reach widespread adoption.

Education

Shaun has an undergraduate degree in business from the University of Hawaii, a Master of Science in Maritime Management from the Maine Maritime Academy and a Master of Science in Business Logistics from Penn State University. He has taught both logistics and SAP software.

Software Certifications

Shaun has been trained and/or certified in products from i2 Technologies, Servigistics, ToolsGroup and SAP (SD, DP, SNP, SPP, EWM).

Contact

Shaun can be contacted at: shaunsnapp@scmfocus.com

Abbreviations

ERP – Enterprise Resource Planning
MEIO – Inventory Optimization and Multi Echelon Planning Software
S&OP – Sales and Operations Planning
CRM: Customer Relationship Management
APS: Advanced Planning and Scheduling
IBP: Integrated Business Planning
SNP: Supply Network Planning
APO: Advanced Planning and Optimization

Links Listed in the Book by Chapter

Chapter 1:

http://www.scmfocus.com/writing-rules/

http://www.scmfocus.com/

Chapter 2:

http://www.scmfocus.com/sapplanning/2009/07/01/bottleneck-resources/

http://www.scmfocus.com/supplyplanning/2011/10/02/commonly-used-and-unused-constraints-for-supply-planning/

Chapter 6:

http://www.scmfocus.com/demandplanning/2010/07/pivot-forecastingrendersforecast-hierarchies-obsolete/

http://www.scmfocus.com/demandplanning/2011/05/flexible-attributeselection-in-smoothie/

http://www.scmfocus.com/demandplanning/2011/05/a-better-wayofimporting-data-into-forecasting-and-analytic-systems/

http://www.scmfocus.com/demandplanning/2011/05/flexible-attributeselection-in-smoothie/

http://www.scmfocus.com/demandplanning/2011/03/forecastdisaggregation-in-smoothie-vs-sap-dp/

www.ingramcontent.com/pod-product-compliance
Lightning Source LLC
LaVergne TN
LVHW080059070326
832902LV00014B/2321